Full Guide to Being Cocky and Funny

Full Guide to Being Cocky and Funny

INTRODUCTION

This guide is the result of 2 years of research into the best methods to have more power and choice with the opposite sex.

In a nutshell, I put this guide together to help other men do better with women. I think that ultimately what every man wants is to meet that ONE special woman. Unfortunately, you may have to meet dozens, if not hundreds, of women before you'll find "the one". And if you don't have the knowledge and experience to deal properly with women in the first place, odds are you'll blow it when you finally meet that special woman. I've seen it...firsthand.

When the woman of your dreams DOES come around, you're going to have to say and do everything right. Truly spectacular women are few and far between, so you'd better be ready. This guide is designed to give you a comprehensive, user-friendly system in order to be ready when that time comes.

About half the contents of this guide are a compilation of my thinking and experience. The other half are compiled from the excellent material and ideas from:

David DeAngelo www.doubleyourdating.com
Tyler Durden www.realsocialdynamics.com
Swingcat www.realworldseduction.com
Mystery www.mysterymethod.com
Moderated alt.seduction.fast (masf) www.fastseduction.com and the great contributions to that board by Tyler Durden, Style, Mystery, Papa, jlaix, and many others
Cliff's Newsletter www.be-relentless.com
The Don Juan Newsletter www.sosuave.com
Thundercat's Seduction Lair www.thundercatsedutctionlair.com
The Player's Guide from AskMen.com www.playersguide.com
Tony's Lay Guide www.layguide.com
Ross Jeffries Speed Seduction www.seduction.com

Full Guide to Being Cocky and Funny

You can investigate these websites and their material on your own, however with this guide I've done all the work for you, and "trimmed the fat" in their systems to give you the bare bones of what works. Just as I've taken from others, feel free to take what you find herein and adapt it to your own style and needs.

What you'll find different about my guide is that I don't just lay out broad principles and expect people to be able to apply them. It's not enough to just tell a guy to "Say something to her to show that her testing doesn't affect you". He needs to see examples of WHAT to say to communicate that it doesn't affect him. Not only do I provide the "what" to do and say in many situations, but I also often provide some ideas of what to do and say if the situation continues further.

Another thing that's lacking in most systems is a STRUCTURE. I've integrated these techniques into a structure to successfully pick up or seduce a woman. This structure is based on the one espoused by the instructors at Real Social Dynamics, and can be seen described in a video of Papa available on Kazaa and on the WinMX network.

The whole idea of this structure is that regardless of the interaction with a woman, whether it's a 2-minute street pickup or a 2-hour date, there are several phases that you go through for a successful pick-up/seduction:

1. ATTITUDE This is the most important part, and is taken care of BEFORE the interaction. Unless you have the right mindset your efforts at attracting a woman will fail.

2. FIND/OPEN This means preparing yourself, going where the woman is, and opening/approaching her.

3. ATTRACT In this phase, you use techniques to build attraction and sexual tension.

4. QUALIFY This involves showing that you're in the frame of being selective and that you're evaluating HER. Can be something as simple as "You seem cool."

5. RAPPORT This phase involves building trust and rapport through emotionally engaging conversation, cold reading, empathy, etc

6. AMPLIFY In this phase you use techniques to build up the attraction and sexual

tension, to an even higher level.

7. CLOSE This phase involves "sealing the deal" (contact close, meet close, kiss close, or sex close)

As an acronym, this is the A-FOAQRAC plan ("folk-rack" for ease of remembering it). To "phase-shift" means to shift from one of these phases to the next. You don't HAVE to necessarily go through all of these phases to have success with a woman, and you don't have to follow the same order, but ideally you should. Obviously you're going to have to find and open a woman, and some attraction/chemistry will be necessary. You'll also have to close her at some point (unless you're just out to practice your game). The other phases are less important, but still have some bearing.

In any case an important principle is to do the least amount necessary to get to the next phase.

Firstly you need this... Chapter1...

ATTITUDE

1. The Ethics of Seduction Techniques
2. The Stigma of the Pick-Up Artist
3. Knowing What You Want
4. Realize that Women are Sexual Beings
5. A Practical Outlook—For Life
6. The Myth of General Confidence
7. The Power of Beliefs
8. The Most Powerful Belief
9. Controlling Frames and Meta-Frames
10. Controlling Your Physical and Emotional State
11. Applying it All in the Field

This phase is not part of the encounter but instead is something that MUST be addressed before the encounter. The "Inner Game" is EVERYTHING. All of the techniques, strategies, and lines to follow are USELESS unless you've got the right mindset.

Full Guide to Being Cocky and Funny

1. The Ethics of Seduction Techniques

When I started to study pick-up and seduction, a big dilemma I had was whether what I was undertaking was RIGHT. I felt a little dishonest, dare I say SLEAZY, about the whole idea of using "tricks" to improve my chances with women. I also felt like less of a "real man" in seeing I had to resort to them. I realized eventually that such moral dilemmas would have to be worked out in order for me to be congruent, and have any success in the field at all. From what I've seen most of the guys out there are decent, moral people with a conscience, so I think that a lot of people in this game have at some point or another felt this way. I'd like to lay out the thinking that got me over this dilemma, in the hopes that anyone else struggling with the same problem might be able to iron out this kink in their inner game.

First of all, realize that there's nothing wrong with having to learn tactics to meet and seduce women. Most men are absolutely CLUELESS in this area, and it's not entirely their fault. A lot of this has to do with being raised by our mothers, as well as the tendency of men not to seek out help or advice. Women, on the other hand, grow up reading Seventeen magazine and YM, watching soaps, and focusing more on interpersonal relationships than men. By the time they're adults they have a whole array of techniques and strategies to tease, hook, and trap a man. They become MASTERS (mistresses?) of manipulation of the opposite sex. Until the Internet resources we enjoy became available and known, men didn't have anything like Cosmo or Sex In The City to teach them the finer points of meeting and choosing a mate. So the fact that you're learning techniques to be able to deal with their expertise on their level doesn't make you less of a man; it just means that you're catching up to their extensive experience, and leveling the playing field.

Another important step is to remove from your mind any negative connotations with the idea of manipulation. (Credit to Ross Jeffries for getting me thinking about this issue). I believe that all human beings require SOME level of manipulation! Advertising tries to manipulate us to buy soft drinks and the latest clothes. You try to manipulate your friends to go see the movie that YOU want to see. The act of manipulation (and the technology/techniques we use in our case to do it) is morally NEUTRAL; it's just the context under which it's done which makes it good or bad. For example, a salesman manipulates you into buying a product, which is his job. You're happy with the product you bought, and he's happy with the commission he made. Where's the harm?

Full Guide to Being Cocky and Funny

You may also have a problem assuming the techniques and the seduction mindset into your personality, thinking that the methods just aren't YOU and that it presents a "fake" you. Consider this: Let's say you're an engineer. Were you an engineer from birth? Of course not. You had to study math and the sciences in high school, and then pursue higher education to get an engineering degree. It took years but now, YOU are an engineer! And so it is with seduction. If you continue learning new material and field-testing it, eventually it'll become YOU. Realize also that a woman out on the town in flashy, skin- tight clothes and painstakingly-applied makeup is NOT "her". "Her" is the girl who 5 hours earlier was standing in front of her mirror miserable and panicking because she was having a bad hair day. The heels, the make-up, the confident air, ALL of these are tools to make herself appear more attractive to the opposite sex. So don't feel guilty or awkward when using "personality tools" of your own to achieve the same result.

Most importantly, if you value yourself and your life as being important in the grand scheme of things (and you SHOULD, since it's YOUR life), then you should also believe that you deserve the very best that life has to offer. This includes finding the very best MATE that you can find. If learning seduction techniques and applying them can improve your chances of meeting the best woman for you out there, then mastering them is one of the noblest undertakings of your life.

2. The Stigma of the Pick-Up Artist

The words "Pick-Up Artist", "Getting picked up", "A quick pick-up", etc all have a NEGATIVE stigma attached to them. The implication is that they're something sneaky or dishonest about approaching women with the intention of meeting them, and that any man that does this is obviously a sleaze ball. The word "seduction" also has a negative connotation as well, somewhat along the lines of "conning" a woman into sleeping with you. Lastly, there's the word "Player", denoting a man who plays games with women's hearts to get them
into bed.

Before you do anything else, you MUST remove from your mind any negative stigmas attached to these concepts. These stigmas are total bullshit, stuff left over from more prudish times when women were chaste and men were seen as being up to no good, trying to "deflower" the poor, poor, victim/woman.

Full Guide to Being Cocky and Funny

Let's be clear here: Although the word "pick-up artist/PUA" or "picking up" is used throughout this guide, to "pick up" someone, is to MEET them. People have been meeting their mates in one way or another since the human race began. In almost all cases it involved one or both of the parties sticking their neck out to meet and form a connection. Now of course, there are exceptions. It's nice that your uncle met his wife because they sat together in a college class, or that a beautiful woman accidentally spilled coffee on your friend and they're now happily married, but this is rare. Out of all the women on the planet, what do you think the REAL chances are that you'll meet your perfect mate completely by chance? Not good at all (although Hollywood movies and Oprah will have you believe otherwise).

In fact, the "pick-up artist" deserves MORE respect than someone who "stumbled onto his wife". The pick-up artist, the one relentlessly and fearlessly approaching women, meeting a LOT of people and forming a LOT of connections, is actively making an effort at finding the right woman for him (or at least building a skill-set so that he knows what to do when he finds her). He's grabbing his cojones and going out on the hunt. In caveman times this guy would be the one dragging a buffalo home for supper every night, while the rest would wait for an old buffalo to fall over dead at their feet.

The word "seduction" also has a negative stigma, most likely because of the outdated beliefs in feminine chastity. The truth is that women WANT to be seduced. It's up to the man to take the lead, and up to the woman to playfully resist and throw up obstacles, and give in if the man is successful in demonstrating his value to her. It's part of courtship, and always will be.

As for the word "player", granted there are men out there who "play" women, as in con them into bed through lies and false promises. But just as fish have their mating dances, peacocks have their displays, and elk have their masculine posturing, humans have their own courtship rituals. The slang for these rituals is "The Game", and everyone out to meet a mate is technically "player" in the game. Women play games all the time, but it's not malicious—they're just playing their part in that courtship ritual. We men need to play the game too, and this doesn't necessarily involve breaking a woman's heart or tricking her. It just means playing our role in the courtship ritual with our own techniques and knowledge of the rules.

As with any social situation, it all comes down to this: Be fair in your dealings with people, and you'll be beyond reproach. Don't let a silly label make you feel guilty.

Full Guide to Being Cocky and Funny

3. Knowing What You Want

Before you can work towards a goal, you have to properly define what that goal is. So if you're looking for your ideal woman, you have to decide what qualities and values she's going to have to have to be the one.

You have to come up with your own, but these are mine. KNOW what you want and you'll be more likely to get it.

Adventurous Spontaneous Emotionally Strong Up For A Challenge Bisexual
Good Wit (Sarcasm)
Sophistication
Optimist
Not Afraid To Take Chances
Still Has A Little Girl Quality About Her
Anti Values: Drama
Neediness Indecisiveness Flakiness

HOWEVER, no matter how much a woman fits your "criteria", DON'T think about her as a girlfriend. Start by thinking of her as a fun, beautiful, but temporary addition to your life. In other words, just have fun with her, give her no restrictions, don't box her in, don't demand anything of her, don't take anything too seriously, etc. Just laugh with her and have sex with her, take her to movies, be cool around town with her on your arm, etc. If it's going to get serious, it'll happen on its own if you just TAKE IT EASY. Most relationships fail because people get too serious too fast, and build up fantasies of the other person that they can't live up to. The ones that last are the ones where the two parties were at the very least "flirting friends" for a while, or had a physical fling that grew into something more with time.

Beware of women in the "gimme" category, i.e. commitment, amount of time spent, emotional support, talking about what they want to talk about, etc. In other words, THEIR agenda, without considering what you could want. It's as if they assume that just because they give you sex or attention, somehow you as a man now are getting everything you could want and must give them what they want. A woman who'll respect your other needs as well as her own, has the potential to be a long-term match.

Full Guide to Being Cocky and Funny

4. Realize that Women are Sexual Beings

Women love sex as much as men do. The only difference is their TERMS for having it. With this in mind, realize that women are in fact SEXUAL BEINGS. Stop talking to them as if they were fragile little children, or immaculate, perfect angels with no sense of sexuality. Also realize their games are TESTS, to see if you're good enough to get sexually involved with. Enjoy the games, get excited when she "shit-tests" you, because it means she's evaluating you as a potential partner. Women want a man who's more powerful than they are, a man who can overcome her obstacles. So how do you think a woman is going to test for that? She's going to give you shit!

Most importantly of all, don't try to hide the fact that YOU are a sexual being! Women know we want them and love sex, so don't hide your libido completely or make apologies for your desires as a man. Women never apologize or act ashamed for wanting love or emotional fulfillment, so why should you hide the fact that you love sex?

We men often don't realize the sexual power that we have over women. We seem to perceive that women have all the sexual power, but when we realize that women desire men just as much as we desire them, we can take back that sexual power. We have the power to choose who we want to talk to, and we are the ones who take the lead. If choice is power, who has more power in this situation: The woman who chooses one of 20 men who approach her, or one of the men who had 300 women/options in the club and decided to approach HER?

And here's a little-known fact: A woman has a lot more to lose than you do if you don't approach her. She spent a lot of money on her outfit, a lot of time getting ready, putting on makeup, doing her hair, etc. By the time she goes out she may have invested 20 hours in shopping for that perfect outfit and getting prepared. If she gives you a signal and you decide not to approach her, it can be a real blow to her ego. Remember that next time you think her beauty gives her all the sexual power!

5. A Practical Outlook—For Life

Indifference to success or failure is the ultimate power. In fact, it's impossible to define success or failure, because each is contextual and can only be assessed in retrospect. For example, if a woman you've been involved with decides you're not the one for her and dumps you, and you didn't see it coming, does that mean you've failed? In the immediate context of the moment it appears you did. BUT if the next day, to feel better you go out with your single friends and meet the woman of your dreams, did you technically FAIL in the long run? Of course not! If you'd "succeeded" with the other woman, you probably would've missed the opportunity with the new woman of your dreams. You need to stop thinking in terms of success or failure, and start taking this OVERALL view of life, instead of viewing things as separate "bubbles" in your life where success or failure are defined in the moment.

6. The Myth of General Confidence

There is no such thing as "confidence" as a general term. Confidence is context-specific. Let me explain:

Let's say that you're a highly-skilled heart surgeon. After years of schooling and training, and experience in the operating room, you're as confident as it gets on the job. You're tops in your field and you know it. Now, just as you leave the operating room, you go into the waiting room and see that a terrorist has left a nuclear suitcase bomb in the waiting room! There's 2 minutes until it blows, meaning there's no time to call the bomb squad. You open the bomb and see a bunch of wires and parts, and your confidence drops to ZERO as you realize that you're clueless and powerless in this situation.

Suddenly a man in the waiting room sees what you're doing and comes to help you. He calmly reaches into the device, turns a dial and pulls a wire, and the timer on the device stops. He doesn't even look scared! In fact, he looks extremely confident. You ask him how he knew how to stop the bomb and he proudly says "I designed this weapon. I worked for 25 years at Los Alamos building nukes. Turning it off is child's play." Now your heart is still racing at this point and the stress hasn't gone away yet, and all of a sudden you have a heart attack and stop breathing. The nuclear bomb technician has no medical training whatsoever, not even a first aid course. Suddenly HIS confidence drops to ZERO as he realizes that he's clueless and powerless in this situation, and he calls for help.

The above story illustrates my point: There's no such thing as a "confident" person, only a person confident in areas he's very familiar with. If you have no skills and experience dealing with something, you won't have any confidence in dealing with it either!

And so it is with women. If someone is experiencing nervousness or a lack of confidence in dealing with women, it's because they don't have the SKILL-SET or experience for dealing with them. No hypnosis tape, no affirmation program, or Neuro-Linguistic Programming trick will give you instant confidence for dealing with women. The only thing that will give you that confidence is the SKILL-SET of how to deal with women (the point of this guide), and EXPERIENCE in dealing with them (you getting out there and interacting with them, using your skillset).

7. The Power of Beliefs

Strong beliefs set the groundwork for a proper mindset.

You can't control events. Instead, you can always control WHAT THINGS MEAN. You need to communicate to yourself what things mean, in order to control your reaction to them. Nothing in life has any meaning except the meaning you give it! The meaning you give something forms the basis of a belief.

What you believe becomes your reality. When you have beliefs that YOU are the prize—such as "women find me irresistible" or "women just want to use me for sex" your mind begins to find evidence of this in the real world. And the more evidence your mind finds of your beliefs, the stronger they become, and the stronger they become, the more convincing and congruent you'll come off to women.

Does it matter if these beliefs are total bullshit? Of course not! Most of the beliefs we have are wrong anyway, be it the belief that we're not good enough to do A, not smart enough to know B, etc. If you're going to believe things that are wrong, why not adopt a wrong belief that EMPOWERS you instead?

Once adopted, beliefs can take on a life of their own and turn us into a completely new person. Look at a hardcore racist for example: His beliefs are ignorant and ridiculous, but to him they're completely real. His interpretations of his experiences, according to his beliefs, have led him to believe that certain races are better than others, or even that the inferior ones should be wiped out. If a person can adopt such extreme beliefs as those, then having it become your reality that women want you should be a cakewalk. All it takes is the right thoughts and influences, and whether you realize it or not YOU are in COMPLETE CONTROL of these.

8. The Most Powerful Belief

The most important (actually, ESSENTIAL) belief you must have is the belief that YOU are the PRIZE when dealing with women. Believe that BEING WITH YOU IS THE BEST CHOICE THAT A WOMAN CAN MAKE. When you adopt this belief, all your other beliefs about dealing with women fall into place naturally.

When YOU adopt the belief that you're the prize, you communicate it automatically through your words, body language, and behavior. Here are some ways the belief manifests itself:

*   When you approach a beautiful woman, you're not trying to win her over. Instead, you're investigating whether she's good enough to be with you. TYPICAL GUY BEHAVIOR: Guy gets all nervous approaching, worrying if SHE will accept him. Guy tries to prove himself to her.

*   When a woman isn't interested in you, it doesn't bother you one bit because she missed out on YOU. In fact, you feel sorry for her, in that she'll never get to experience being with you. TYPICAL GUY BEHAVIOR: It hurts his self-worth, and he feels sorry for himself, because he'll never have the experience of being with her.

*   If a woman you're involved with decides to leave, it's no big deal because YOU are the prize. Not only is it her loss, but someone better than her will come along shortly. TYPICAL GUY BEHAVIOR: Guy chases the woman, begs her to come back, saying that he'll never meet anyone like her again.

*   You never chase after, plead, beg, supplicate, or try to buy a woman's attention or affection with dinners and gifts. SHE should be the one buying YOU gifts, and trying to win YOU over. TYPICAL GUY BEHAVIOR: Betrays his insecurity by chasing after her, asking how she feels about him, trying to win her affection with gifts, etc.

*   You never get stuck on ONE woman (the scarcity mentality), since you're better than she is anyway—YOU are the prize! TYPICAL GUY BEHAVIOR: Suffers from "One-itis", builds up a huge fantasy in his mind about her, and since he just HAS to get THIS particular girl, he's lost all his power with her.

*   You have a LIFE of your own, the lifestyle of a cool guy full of great friends,

successful people, and good vibes. You stay invested in your hobbies and enjoy your life. If a woman wants to be with you, she has to respect the life you already have. It's YOUR train, and she just gets to ride it. TYPICAL GUY BEHAVIOR: Drops his friends to be with a woman, makes her the center of his universe, drops his hobbies to spend time with her (or worse, makes thinking about her his hobby).

* You date multiple women at once, to determine who's best for you to be with long-term. You expect the BEST mate possible because YOU are the prize, and you can't find the best if you only spend time with and get to know one. You feel much more comfortable approaching women, because if it doesn't work you're still dating other women. TYPICAL GUY BEHAVIOR: Commits to one woman at a time, usually the first to "accept" him, overlooks her glaring faults, "settles" until she dumps him and he wonders
"What did I see in her?"

* You don't accept shitty behavior from women. Since you're the PRIZE, she'd better be treating you properly or she's OUT. TYPICAL GUY BEHAVIOR: Lets girl walk all over him and boss him around, because he thanks his lucky stars that a girl as hot as her has "accepted" him—to him she's the prize.

* No matter how much you grow to like or love her, you imagine that she likes or loves you MORE. Although you're lucky to be with her, she's even luckier to be with you. TYPICAL GUY BEHAVIOR: Guy falls head over heels and lets her "own" him, tells her how lucky he is to be with her, or how he could never live without her.

* When you first meet a woman, whenever she tells you she doesn't like something about you, you see it as HER problem, not yours. TYPICAL GUY BEHAVIOR: Guy gets all self-conscious about whatever it was she pointed out, and either agrees with her or tries to justify himself to get back in her favor.

See the difference? Most typical guy behaviors imply that the woman is the prize. But when you switch things around and assume the role of the prize in your thoughts, words, and actions, you behave much differently. Your behavior will communicate to women that YOU are the prize that she has to win over, without saying it outright. Again, does it matter whether it's true or not that you really ARE the prize? NO! A fat, balding, ugly man who believes he's God's gift to women will have more success with women than a fat, balding, ugly man who's "realistic" and thinks that no woman would be into him given his state. (Funny enough, negative people often justify their negative attitude by claiming to be "realistic"). I'll say it one more time: Whether the belief is true or not means nothing; IT'S HOW STRONGLY THAT BELIEF IS HELD THAT COUNTS. Perception is everything!

9. Controlling Frames and Meta-Frames

For a proper attitude in dealing with women it's very important to understand the concept of FRAMES. Swinggcat explains the concept pretty well in his e-book "Real World Seduction". Here's a paraphrasing of the section on frames:

A "frame" is a general focus or direction that provides an overall guide for thoughts and actions during an interaction. A frame determines the underlying meaning of behaviors and actions. A "meta-frame" is an overall focus or direction that provides a meaning to the interaction. A more general term for frames and meta-frames is the SOCIAL DYNAMIC.

Frames don't exist in objective reality. They're not "real". They only exist inside the skulls of human beings. But they're extremely important in dealing with people.

Generally, when two people's meta-frames are in conflict, the stronger/more assertive meta-frame is dominant.

A woman may or may not buy into your meta-frame. But even if she doesn't, you're conveying that you're unwilling to buy into hers.

How to control the Meta-Frame:

Step 1: Define the meta-frame: If you don't set it, the woman will define it for you, and assert hers.

Here's a way to properly define the underlying meaning of the interaction:

1. You are the PRIZE.
2. She's trying to get you to like her or trying to win you over—whether it be in the sense of attraction, acceptance, or validation.
3. She wants you so bad that she's trying to make you sleep with her.
4. The both of you are going to sleep together, but only if she lives up to your standards and expectations.

Full Guide to Being Cocky and Funny

Step 2: Assume the meta-frame in advance

Assume before even talking to her that the underlying meaning of all her behaviors and actions when you do talk to her will fit into your meta-frame.

Step 3: Set frames that imply the meta-frame. Some ways to do this:

1. Frame one or more of her actions, behaviors, or things about her as meaning that she's not good enough for you or can't handle you (implies you're the prize)
2. Frame one or more of her actions as her being interested or trying to pursue YOU
3. Frame one or more of her behaviors or actions as her being a little crazy (refuse to buy into it)
4. Frame one or more of her behaviors, actions, or something about her as meaning that she lacks class
5. Frame one or more of her behaviors, actions, or something about her as meaning that she's a dork
6. Accuse her of not really living the life that she wants to live, or accuse her of being envious of you
7. Frame one or more of her behaviors, actions, or something about her as meaning that she's a little creepy
8. Frame some of her behaviors, actions, or things about her as meaning that she's a sleaze ball.
9. Frame some of her behaviors and actions as being rude and insensitive

Notice that many of these frames are the frames that women set with guys. So, you're taking the frames they use to turn guys into frustrated, pathetic beggars, and using them against them.

Attempt at all times to do this in a humorous way. When women are laughing, their guard is down and they're more apt to go along with the frames you're setting.

10. Controlling Your Physical and Emotional State

YOU are the only one responsible for how you feel. Other people don't make us feel anything. It's OUR OWN interpretations of their words and behavior that affect us.

Full Guide to Being Cocky and Funny

Controlling how you feel is crucial. It's up to you to remain emotionally calm. Women count on us for this, and thank us for it when they go nutty. It's the MAN'S responsibility to be in control of hi emotions. Women are NOT attracted to weepy little wimps. I'm not saying you can't show emotion, but don't be provoked to feel an emotion by another person that you don't CHOOSE to have. Every woman out there has her own insecurities and fears. Remember that you have the advantage of strategies and logic on your side, and all you need to do is CONTROL YOUR STATE!

You are going to have to STOP getting emotional when women try to make you angry, sad, or upset. These are all tests by women, and you will FALL right into the trap by getting all worked up. You are going to have to STOP falling for all their games, dramatic behavior, and attempts to control you through your fear of losing them. Women DESIRE a man who is BEYOND their control, beyond their attempts to make him do anything, or to make him upset. The message is if you put up with her crap, how can you protect her? A dominant man allows a woman to feel safe and protected.

So how do you control your state? How do you stay calm when a woman is yelling at you for stupid shit, or when she just dissed you in front of the entire party?

Positively interpreting things is one way. At some point in your life you've probably been in a situation where something embarrassing or negative happened to you, and someone said "One day you'll look back on this and laugh." And you probably did! Well when you find yourself in a shitty situation today, why not laugh at it TODAY? Why wait for someday? Also, think of how terrible something may have seemed when it happened to you years ago, and how it means nothing to you now. When something negative happens to you today, why not have it mean nothing to you TODAY as well? This can be done through positive interpretation, a RE-FRAMING of the "negative" situation.

Here's another method for controlling your state:

Your physical and emotional states are closely tied together. For example, when someone is depressed, what do they look like physically? Often they're slumped over with poor posture, taking short steps, their head's down, and they have a sad look on their face. And when someone's happy or excited they bounce around and they're more animated.

The fact that there's a link between the physical and the emotional is good news for controlling our state. When you find yourself slouched over and unfocused, you can sit up straight with good posture and breathe deeply, and you'll find yourself more alert and able to concentrate. When you find yourself worried about something, you can stand tall, look up at the ceiling, smile a big smile, and hold it (in fact, it's hard to stay in ANY negative state in this position). You can breathe deeply and slowly to reduce anxiety and fear. And when a woman is going crazy and giving you problems, you can take a deep breath, smile and narrow your eyes at her, and slowly cross your arms.

11. Applying it All in The Field

It's extremely important to adopt the attitudes above before going out to apply what you learn in the field. Although the techniques described later in this guide are VERY effective for what they're supposed to do, if you don't have the right mindset they'll work poorly. Many newcomers to this stuff want to learn the tricks and techniques only, and this is a bad idea. Learning only the pick-up techniques while keeping your old attitudes is like learning fancy jiu-jitsu techniques while staying seriously out of shape. You may learn a great arm-lock or strike that could end a fight in seconds, but if you don't have the strength and conditioning to apply it, the technique itself is useless.

Chapter 2...

FIND/OPEN PHASE

<u>Highlights:</u>

1. Preparing yourself
2. Dealing with the fear of rejection
3. Warming up
4. Finding "Targets"
5. Opening
6. Opening Groupsets
7. Bitch Shield Destroyers
8. Boyfriend Destroyers
9. Objection Destroyers
10. Specific Circumstances Openers
11. Wingman Strategies
12. Phase-Shifting to ATTRACT

"Pick-up is the art of conveying who you are in the shortest time possible." and "Pickup is VERBAL FOREPLAY" --Tyler Durden, Cliff's List

You hear guys complaining all the time that it's hard to meet women. But are they even TRYING? Usually when guys say "It's so hard to meet women" what they mean is that it's hard to have a woman just fall in their lap, the way people meet in the movies. They expect the girl of their dreams to be hired at the office and partnered up with them on their next sales project. They expect to hang out with the same circle of friends they've had for years and suddenly one of their friends will have this great new available female friend to introduce them to.

The truth is that your dream girl is out there, waiting to meet a guy like you. BUT TO

Full Guide to Being Cocky and Funny

MEET HER, YOU'RE GOING TO HAVE TO LEAVE THE HOUSE! You have to take the initiative and get out there, and MAKE MOVES. The odds of your dream girl being a door-to-door saleswoman who knocks on your door to sell you the latest vacuum cleaner are slim to none. You'll have to stick your neck out, risk rejection, and build new bonds with people. You are going to have to be SOCIAL. To even have a chance at finding her, you're going to have to FIND a woman, and you're going to have to OPEN an interaction with her.

1. Preparing yourself

Before you go out to find and open women, you need to prepare yourself for it. There are three components to this preparation: Mental, physical, and style.

MENTAL—APPROACH PHILOSOPHY

Aside from having the proper attitude for dealing with women, you need to have specific attitudes ingrained for approaching total strangers.

When approaching, just walk up to the woman and say FUCK IT. Keep yourself in the frame that you're just goofing around and you don't need to do well, just as long as you do it and have fun with it. Even if you don't get the girl, you got to practice your skill-set and learned how to do it better next time. There is NO downside!

Often the single woman is very lonely. Not many guys seriously ask hot women on dates, and when they're asked they'll take advantage of it even if you're not their knight in shining armour. You have to understand that even though many women receive attention constantly, they don't actually get asked out on dates. This can be for many reasons and the initial one to come to mind is that all of the guys thought she'd say no. They may think she's too good for them and she may not come across as the approachable type. SO GO FOR IT!

Be super-confident, presupposing that she wants your company and will give her number to you...Or more.

Full Guide to Being Cocky and Funny

PHYSICAL

It's not necessary to be a gorgeous hunk of male to have success approaching women. But if you have some physical flaw that you could go and take care of, it's just another strike against you. Just like a baseball player can have two strikes against him and still hit a home run, you can be unshaven and overweight and still get a number. But why risk it?

Strive to keep yourself looking your best physically at all times. This doesn't mean being TOO concerned about your appearance; it means keeping your nails clean and short, your hands callus-free as much as possible, your "UNI-BROW" groomed, and your hair trimmed at least every 3 weeks to keep it neat. Be clean-shaven (unless you're going for the unshaven look), and keep your body clean! This means showering before going out, and controlling body odor with a good deodorant. Brush your teeth and chew on mint gum to keep your breath fresh.

Get enough sleep every night so that you're in top shape for approaching. Avoid drugs and alcohol that will leave you with mood swings, or tired and bloodshot eyes. If you absolutely have to take a couple drinks to loosen up on a night out on the town, keep it reasonable. Avoid beer if you can, because it leaves your breath smelling bad and makes it obvious you've been drinking. Vodka has a tendency to be undetectable on someone's breath a few minutes after ingestion, so go with that.

You should also attempt to keep yourself in shape as much as possible. Look into proper eating habits and stay physically active. A complaint that many guys have is that they don't have enough TIME to work out. The way around this is to focus more on QUALITY in your workouts rather than quantity of exercise. Get in the gym, be intense, lift heavy weights slowly, do intense cardio, and go home and rest. Doing things this way, you can get the results from 2-3 workouts a week that someone might get working out 5 times a week while taking it easy, resting a lot between sets, etc.

Pay attention to your posture. If you find yourself hunched over a lot, make a habit of holding your chest up. This alone has an amazing effect on your posture, forcing your head up and your shoulders back.

You can also help your success by going out and doing certain things. If you're pale, go to the tanning salon once every week or two to give your skin a dash of color. See the dentist to have your teeth whitened, or pick up a kit on eBay to do it yourself. If you're unusually hairy, keep your back and neck waxed, or undergo laser hair removal treatments.

STYLE

Make an effort to keep up with the latest styles. Look at ads in men's magazines like Maxim, Stuff, or FHM (or GQ if you're older than say, 35) to get an idea of what looks are in. Then go about looking for similar styles, and picking up the items you like best to build your wardrobe. If your budget is a problem, try on the clothing in the store, and when you know your size for that designer/company go onto eBay and look for things in your size. Things needn't be brand-name either; go buy cheap clothes if you want, and just get rid of the indicators that the clothes are cheap (remove the leather tab on the back of cheap jeans, for example). Really, some people will tell you to buy expensive, well-made clothes that will last you years. That's not the point here. You want cheap clothes that will last you a year or two, that you can replace the following year. Workmanship won't be a big deal either; unless someone is scrutinizing your clothes carefully, they won't notice that the seam of your pants is a little crooked around the ankle, for example. Although women DO tend to notice details (like if your shoes are scuffed or your belt fits your pants), they won't be going over the workmanship of your clothes with a magnifying glass. And by the time your clothes are off and she can see the tags identifying it as cheap crap, you're already where you want to be!

Of course, if you've got the money to spend, go for quality AND style. "Peacocking" Women tend to wear a lot of clothing that is functionally useless, impractical, or downright uncomfortable. They'll wear high heels, pointless accessories, boots that go up to their knees, and skimpy tops in not-so-warm weather. They'll get tattoos and navel piercings and other odd things. This is SEXUAL ORNAMENTATION to catch attention from men (and to compete with other women—but that's another matter entirely).

What most people don't realize is that sexual ornamentation WORKS BOTH WAYS. This has led to Mystery's theory of PEACOCKING. Just like a male peacock spreads his feathers and shows them off to catch female attention, a male human can display clothing and accessories that catch the attention of human females.

Mystery's motto on peacocking is that IT'S BETTER TO BE LOOKED OVER THAN OVERLOOKED. To this end Mystery himself goes out intending to get looked over. Already standing at 6'5" tall, he wears shoes with 6-inch platforms, and a funky black fur hat with aviator goggles wrapped around it. He paints his fingernails black, and even uses this as an opinion opener by slapping his hand down on the table and saying "What are your first impressions of black nails?" He's been known too to wear a T-shirt with a LED electronic sign on the chest that scrolls "Mystery" in red letters. He's very hard to miss, his style of dress definitely shows personality, and women get a genuine curiosity about him.

Obviously you don't have to go this far to get attention. You can just take steps to be noticed and stand out, and not be just another Calvin Klein Clone in the club. Here are some examples on how to "peacock":

*   Get highlights put in your hair

*   Get piercings (loops in both ears, or eyebrow, lip, nose, tongue)

*   Accessorizing!

o   Wear funky sunglasses (including clear ones you can wear in the club)

o   Wear a watch that stands out (BIG links or wristband/cuff-style, unusual style, etc). I have a Diesel watch with a HUGE, shiny stainless steel wristband, and it never fails to get noticed.

o   Wear several rings

o   Wear a silver bracelet or neck chain, etc.

o   If you have a small cell phone, don't hide it in a case or in your pocket. Instead, accessorize it with an original or flashy faceplate (eBay has some odd ones) and hang it around your neck from a plumb chain or cord.

o   If you tuck in your shirts, get a belt with a buckle that draws attention. This doesn't necessarily mean some big western buckle the size of a dinner plate, but one that's flashy or has a strange shape.

*   If you have muscles, show them off! A lot of big guys are self-conscious of their bodies and try to cover them up. If you've worked hard for the body you have, wear SLIGHTLY fitted shirts that display your build. Just like a nice set of cleavage will catch male attention, a muscular chest or

pair of arms displayed will also turn female heads. I say "slightly" because you shouldn't try TOO hard. Just like a woman dressed like a prostitute screams out that she's starved for attention, if you have an "in your face" way of showing your muscles it'll look insecure. If your T- shirts are so tight that you need help getting them on and off, or you put oil on your arms when you go out in a sleeveless top... you're trying too hard.

*   Wear some funky shoes or boots

*   Wear bright colors that grab attention! For example, if you have a choice between buying a shirt in white or in red, go for the red.

*   Buy a lighter that shoots a green or blue flame, then adjust it so that the flame burns high. You get extra peacocking value if the lighter itself

glows a certain color when lit. eBay is great for finding little gadgets like these.

*   Carry an out-of-the-ordinary pen, either something flashy and chromed like a

Full Guide to Being Cocky and Funny

Fisher Space Pen, or something quirky. For example there are pens available that look like syringes with liquid in them. If you don't have the room in your pockets to carry a pen, saw a golf pencil in half with a filet knife and carry the tiny pencil in your wallet. ALWAYS CARRY SOMETHING TO WRITE WITH!

Occasionally a woman might test you on the way you dress, or another guy might make fun of you. You can deal with these challenges using techniques outlined in the ATTRACT section of this guide.

Peacocking is the driving force behind a guy taking a $10,000 car and sinking $10,000 into it to customize it with a flashy paint job, shiny mag wheels, noisy exhaust, etc. It's also why guys will install $2,000 sound systems in their cars ("Boomcars") so that they can broadcast to 5 city blocks that they listen to the latest, coolest music. Unfortunately doing stuff like this is a bad investment for attracting a woman's attention, for the following reasons:

*   Since your car is what's drawing the attention, from a peacocking perspective you're naked when you step out of it and actually go somewhere on foot. Unless you're into picking up fast food cashiers at a drive-thru, or specifically targeting the women who go to import car meets, your car won't help your game when it's all YOU.

*   When you're blasting your music so that no one has any choice about listening to it, most of the people around, including women, will automatically be annoyed with you because they're forced to listen to it. Peacocking with clothing and accessories is PASSIVE—no one is FORCED to look at you if they don't like the way you look.

* $10,000 sunk into you car to turn heads, or $300 spent in wardrobe and accessories to turn heads. See my point?

*   Remember what I said about trying too hard? Well if you put a small fortune into showing off, people will think you're trying too hard. A lot of women have a nickname for expensive, show-off cars: "Penis Extensions"

* If you DO happen to catch some hottie's POSITIVE attention with your noisy, flashy car, what can you do? When the sidewalks outside the clubs are busy, the street is busy too, and parking is scarce. You can double-park and get out (which will promptly get you a ticket since police usually foot patrol the clubbing areas); you can cat-call her through your window (REEEEALLY cool); or you can temporarily stop, stay in the car, and wave her over like a hooker. You're very limited with what you can do.

I'm not saying that having a nice car won't help you with women. Obviously if you go to pick her up for a coffee meeting in a custom car, fully detailed, it'll come off better than if you picked her up in a rusty Ford Pinto. Just don't get the idea that a flashy car, all tricked out, is going to let you pull more women.

Props

Props can really help you out. Sometimes a woman may want to initiate a conversation with YOU, and if you have something on you worth commenting on she'll have her "in". It can be anything unusual, from carrying a 2 foot-long salami over your shoulder, to holding a Chinese fan, to wearing a T-shirt that says "I'm the Italian Your Mother Warned You About" (I actually have this shirt by the way, and it's great on days I feel like coming across very cocky). I know a guy who wears a black T-shirt with "TESTOSTERONE" written across the chest in bright yellow letters. This shirt never fails to get comments from women, usually in the form of testy comments (which is not a bad thing; a test is an ideal "in" to a conversation).

2. Dealing with the fear of rejection

Women get approached all the time, and they get approached by men MUCH scarier than you! As long as you don't act threatening or like a nervous stalker you'll get a good reception, or at worst a polite refusal. If you don't, then that's HER problem, not yours!

Full Guide to Being Cocky and Funny

Always keep in mind that just because you're approaching a woman, it doesn't give her the right to be rude to you. If she rejects you gracefully, eject gracefully. But if she blows you off with an insult, then it's open season on her ego! Smile at her like she's funny and use some condescending comment like "That's cute" or "You had a hard childhood, didn't you?" Whatever you do, DON'T get mad and call her a bitch. First, this is what every guy does, and it just makes you look like another insecure loser bitter at rejection. Second, never forget that your next target may be watching! If you deal with a cold rejection in a cocky way and don't let it faze you, it says a lot about you, in a good way.

If you're having a lot of trouble approaching, the Deliberate Rejection Exercise is the quickest way to get over your fear of approaching hot women. With the DRE, you GO IN WITH THE *INTENTION* OF GETTING REJECTED! Be totally honest and ASK FOR IT! I call this the Deliberate Rejection Exercise (DRE). Here's what I mean: Go somewhere for an afternoon, somewhere far from what would be a future regular pickup ground for you (like a mall on the other side of town). Go at a time when you know there will be a lot of hot women there. With a smile, walk up to a 9 or 10 and say the following: "Hi, I have this FEAR of rejection that I really need to get over. So I need you to just REJECT ME as hard and as cold as possible, so I can get used to it. Go ahead, REJECT ME!" If she ignores you, go C&F: "Is that the BEST you can do? Ignore me? Come on, you can do better than that! Say something MEAN!" If she just giggles or thinks you're putting her on: "What are you laughing for? I mean it!! Be cruel!" When she finally does blow you off badly, thank her and tell her "Only 36 more rejections to go, I have a target of 50". This routine has two beneficial effects:

First, it doesn't matter if you're nervous when you're approaching since your whole point is to get rejected anyway. If you look nervous and blow it, THAT'S THE POINT! Just add it to your "rejection target" of 50 or whatever number you have as a goal. It doesn't matter because after a few times your nervousness will go away, you'll be enjoying the game, and you'll have no fear at all approaching a hot woman cold. On top of this, you'll see that rejection by a 10 isn't that bad, and you can actually make fun of it. Now, contrast this with approaching while trying NOT to get rejected: You get all nervous worrying about getting rejected, and since you're nervous you creep the girl out and she rejects you anyway, which really doesn't help your nervousness the next time you try.

Full Guide to Being Cocky and Funny

Second, it conditions you to approach total female strangers (attractive ones) with a cocky & funny attitude. Throughout the entire routine above, you're being playful. Too many men are afraid to look stupid and thus stay serious and "smooth" around attractive women. Without a base of experience horsing around with hotties, C&F approaches and routines, when eventually used, will seem forced. The woman will pick up that you're uncomfortable and you'll blow it.

When you do the DRE, don't be surprised when half the women you say it to are speechless. You'll see some of them with the look of a deer caught in the headlights, since they've probably NEVER been approached by a guy ASKING to get blown out. It's just so far outside their reality. If you're lucky she might even find it cute, and you'll have yourself a 10-friend! Not a bad thing considering she could introduce you to all her hot friends.

The DRE can be used a couple times as a great warm-up before actual serious PU sessions as well, no matter how experienced you are.

3. Warming Up

Before going out to open "targets", you should warm up psychologically to get into the right state of mind. You can't expect to be thinking about your bills and your grades and your ex bothering you, then immediately jump into a fun, confident mindset when you see a woman you want to meet. After a decent amount of experience you'll be able to snap yourself into state instantly, but don't count on it right away.

What's the best way to warm up? The DRE is one, but the best way by far is by talking to other people! Call male and female friends and joke around with them. Talk to people on the way to the venue you're headed to. Ugly girls, other guys, doormen, street bums, cashiers, taxi drivers, they're all great to talk to for warming up. Be cool with them, talk to them as if they were old friends, and bring up certain topics to see if any of them bomb. Better you learn during your warm-up that a topic is uninteresting or stupid, than later when you're talking to your target. How long it takes to warm up depends on your state when you go out, your experience, etc, but you'll know when you're ready.

Listening to music before going out can get you into state too. You'll have your own ideas about what motivates you to go out and pick up, but here are my choices:

Jimi Hendrix—Foxy Lady (gets me into state and gives me a playful attitude with women)

Janet Jackson—All for You (It's a woman telling a guy not to be shy and to move in and pick her up! It doesn't get any more encouraging than this one)

4. Finding "Targets"

This may seem like an elementary statement but...YOU HAVE TO GO WHERE THE WOMEN ARE! Too many guys cheat themselves out of meeting great women because they avoid the venues where they hang out. They go to sports bars over coffee shops, take golf lessons over Latin dance lessons, go to hardcore gyms over health clubs, they avoid malls, etc.

Get over the idea that an activity or place is "GAY". Yoga may not be the manliest of sports, but it's great cardio-vascular exercise and the classes are usually 28 women and 2 guys. Aerobics classes may look gay to you, but you'll be in a room with mostly young women, all clad in spandex and doing stretches we can only PRAY to see in a strip club. Why not get involved with one of these activities instead of getting your cardio in on a boring treadmill or Stairmaster?

As for hobbies, learning to dance Salsa Merengue or country dancing might look gay to you, but the majority of the people in the class are young women, and the instructor will be forcing people to change partners frequently. Women will literally be FORCED to meet you, and they'll be holding their bodies against you the whole time. You're in an ideal position to run game on them.

Full Guide to Being Cocky and Funny

If you're not into clubs, then coffee shops, health food restaurants, new age/esoteric conventions, health clubs, street festivals, and shopping malls are all excellent places to meet single women. And don't make the mistake of avoiding these places at peak hours. People tend to avoid crowds, but the fact is that if there are more people in a certain place, the law of averages dictates that there's going to be more desirable women there too. If you end up waiting a little bit for a machine at a health club, or in line at a coffee shop, so what? Maybe you'll end up next to an attractive woman and be able to strike up a conversation. You need to get out there.

By the way, a pick-up artist saying he "doesn't do clubs" is like a hockey player saying "I don't do arenas", or a baseball player saying "I don't do stadiums". To really be a successful PUA you HAVE to work clubs and bars. They're the arena where the game is played. Women walking down the street or sitting in a coffee shop may be easier targets with less competition around, but they aren't intentionally there to meet guys. In clubs and bar settings they are! DESPITE what many of them claim. Even those going out for "a night with the girls" are going out with friends who are looking to meet guys. And those who are claiming to go out just to "dance and have fun" aren't ruling out meeting a nice guy. The number of women in clubs who are married or have serious boyfriends and are off-limits, are actually very few.

If you REALLY can't go into clubs because you have asthma and can't take the smoke, or loud music gives you a headache, or you get fed up of people bumping into you, fine. At least go walk along the main clubbing strip and open groups of women walking along or standing in line. Obviously all those women in the club have to walk along that sidewalk to get there in the first place, so why not meet them there? Here are some reasons why this is a good idea:

*   Since they're not in the club yet they probably haven't got their "bitch shields" up. They'll be less likely to blow you off or be rude.

*   There will be less competition. The guys IN the club will have a few drinks in them and will have more balls to approach the women. On the street though, they usually won't be ready to do a serious approach...leaving them all for you!

*   If you catch her before she goes into the club, you'll be the FIRST guy she met that night. You'll stick out in her mind the day after, especially

if you came off cool, and afterwards the guys in the club all approached her like losers. It'll provide more contrast for your value when you call her after.

*   Conversely, if you catch a group of women as they're LEAVING a club and there are no guys with them, odds are they didn't meet anyone THAT spectacular and they're leaving in a frustrated state. Here's your chance to demonstrate your value and salvage their night out.

*   Aside from the guys in the Boomcars driving by, there's no loud music out on the sidewalk. You can say anything and have it be understood, without having to repeat yourself 3 times or scream in a girl's ear.

If you happen to have a good-looking photo of yourself (either a snapshot or professionally done photo) you can also put a profile on the Internet and meet women that way. You'll need to be somewhat attractive for this to work, since regardless of how good your profile is, it'll be your picture that makes or breaks you. Internet dating is great for people who are shy or lazy when it comes to going out and meeting women, or who don't have much time. The down side is that a lot of women don't have a picture up, so it's a real crapshoot. You don't know if you're sending a message to a bitter fat girl, or a gorgeous exotic dancer. Also, since it costs money to send messages on most dating networks, it can get pretty expensive. Meeting women is a numbers game sometimes, but with the Internet it's extreme. If it costs $2 to send someone an email or start an IM chat session, and they don't reply back, or end up being warpigs when they send you their photos, it can really hurt your wallet after a while.

5. Opening

The most important principle in opening is to follow the "3-seconds rule" at all times. This basically means as soon as you see a woman you want to meet, within 3

Full Guide to Being Cocky and Funny

SECOND S you move in and open her. This has two very powerful benefits:

In 3 seconds you don't have time to get nervous. Most guys hesitate and talk themselves out of opening a woman because their insecurities take over. Even if they actually manage to kick their own asses to go and approach, by that time they're so nervous from over-thinking it that they'll probably blow the interaction. If you approach in 3 seconds, the hard part is over before you even have a chance to make excuses, and you'll avoid becoming sweaty, nervous, etc.

If a woman sees you hesitating to approach her, you'll look insecure and you'll lose value in her eyes. By moving in within 3 seconds, you look confident and show no hesitation.

The downside of the 3-seconds rule is that it leaves you very little time to think of an opener. This is why it's important to have an arsenal of all-purpose openers committed to memory (opinion openers are best for this). Another way around this is to enter a venue looking for openers rather than looking for targets. This way by the time you start looking for targets to approach, you already have an opener or two in mind that would suit the situation or venue.

Approach Invitation (AI)

Approach Invitation is any indication that a woman has a desire for you to open her. Flirting, maintained eye contact, looking at you and then giggling to her girlfriends, etc. Approach invitation isn't always necessary for a successful approach, so don't wait for it. But having it certainly beats a cold approach. Your odds are much better when you approach a woman who gave you AI. "Proximity AI" is when a woman moves herself within easy opening distance of you. For example, the entire bus could be empty, but she takes the seat across from you. This is the closest you'll usually get to a woman opening you. A woman who wants you to open her will put herself in a spot where you'll notice her, and she's easily accessible.

Opening Body Language

Full Guide to Being Cocky and Funny

COLD APPROACHES: You spot a chick you want. Now the most important thing is how you FACE her. You roll up sideways or diagonally, and you don't face her UNTIL she is facing YOU. That means if she's turned totally away from you, you literally TURN YOUR NECK ENTIRELY BACKWARDS while you talk, and ONLY turn when she turns. Then, as she says stuff that she PERCEIVES as you being impressed by, you THEN turn to face her. This causes her to have the perception that 1) you aren't needy/desperate/lame 2) she said something WORTH you staying. Give her the impression that you're only staying to talk because SHE said something that interested you to stay. Again, do this by ONLY turning once she is turning FIRST. The only exception is doing little tests, like turning quickly towards her, to SEE if she'll BITE and turn herself.

On eye contact/"Warm" approaches (with AI): Real pick-up artists never stare. They lock eye contact. There's a difference between staring and locking eye contact. When you look at a woman, here is what you do. Lock eye contact with her. Don't blink. Don't look at her friend. Pick one eye and don't let go.

You only get one chance at this. Don't give up. Don't smile. Don't say anything. You're telling her that you're interested in her and you're not intimidated by her. Then leave it up to her. You will be amazed at the staring capability that women posses. If she smiles, you smile. If she says Hi, you say Hi. Then you reward her and make your move. You must learn to keep eye contact until SHE breaks it.

Avoid "Hen Pecking", leaning just your head in to hear a woman talk while your body stays square. Move your body into it and get close. Tall and/or built guys need to be more on the side, hip-to-hip rather than facing to avoid intimidating the girl.

Introducing Yourself

When first meeting a woman, don't introduce yourself to her or ask her name. Either one communicates eager interest, which you shouldn't do right away. Instead, wait for HER to ask your name or introduce herself to you, then say:

"It's a pleasure for you to meet me, (name)" (While shaking hand)

Full Guide to Being Cocky and Funny

Only THEN give YOUR name. If she's asking you your name, it's an indicator of interest and an attempt to build rapport—a good thing!

Deflecting the "Pickup Artist"/PUA stigma

If at any point you find your target accusing you of trying to "pick her up", you need to reframe the interaction. Show that you aren't trying to do a pick-up, but simply meet her and see what she's like.

(That's good...that's the best "pick-up" line I've ever heard) "That's not a "pick- up" line... it's an "I WANT TO MEET YOU LINE!"

"I don't "pick up" women...I MEET them."

"For this to be a pickup/pickup line, first I'd have to be INTERESTED in you." Say this with a cocky smirk. This one is usually best for the real hard-ass bitches. If she happens to ask "Well, are you?" pause a few seconds while looking at her, then say "I'm still trying to figure that out".

"I'm NOT picking you up. I'm trying to get to know you to SEE if you're worth picking up." Again, make sure she sees a mischievous smile on your face.

(Have you done this to like a hundred women or something?) "Nope, I've only done this to a thousand." (When women accuse you of player behavior, don't squirm. Instead escalate it). OR "How many women have you done this to?" You reply "THOUSANDS" or "Do you mean just today, or this week?"

(Do you do this to every girl?) "Only the ones who ask silly questions."

Full Guide to Being Cocky and Funny

How many girls do you do this to? "Why? Do you wanna meet girls? Do you want me to show you how?"

WHAT MAKES A GOOD OPENER?

Let there be no doubt: When you approach an attractive woman and open her, she KNOWS you want to sleep with her. You're NOT fooling her. She knows you don't just go up to ugly old ladies and say "Nice purse", or walk up to ugly, deformed bums on street corners and say "Hi!" So don't pretend that you're just out to "make conversation" or just kill time. The KEY to pulling off a successful approach is to signal through your body language, voice tone, and verbal communication that YES you want to sleep with her, but that you DON'T REALLY CARE whether you do or not...or that you're not really sure yet if she's worth it.

Now, on the subject of verbal communication (your opener), there are two main categories of openers: DIRECT and INDIRECT. Direct would be something that communicates outright "I'm interested in you", and Indirect would be an opener that leaves ambiguity in the interaction, leaving some doubt in her mind that you're trying to pick her up—meaning that even though she knows you want to sleep with her, she can't tell yet if that's the reason you're talking to her at the moment.

Whichever style you choose, the openers you use must be ORIGINAL. A study conducted in New York City showed that the average woman was approached 37 times per day by male strangers interested in meeting her. (Now that's the "average", so imagine the attention a really HOT woman must get). Most of these guys use UNoriginal approaches like just saying "Hi" or "Yo baby, what's up?" Or worse, they make a comment on some part of her anatomy. If YOU were an attractive woman, and you heard crap like that 37 times a day, what would you do? You'd start to AUTOMATICALLY ignore them and get turned off by it. Think of the last time you walked downtown in a big city, and remember how many bums approached you asking for change. Odds are before one of them even opened his mouth, you were all primed to say "No" or just plain ignore him as if he wasn't there. It was an automatic response because you're used to behaving like that in the presence of a bum after being approached for change so many times. Now what happens when you see a bum with a witty sign with him, or a decrepit-looking animal beside him, or with a really bad sob story, or one who has a very friendly, charismatic approach? A lot of the time it breaks your pattern and you find yourself giving him change. Likewise, using an unoriginal opener that a woman's heard a million times will trigger her automatic response, and she'll dismiss you, BUT using an original approach will break her pattern and her automatic response will be disarmed.

Another thing you have to watch for is that your opener not be DUMB. Don't ask something like "Nice shoes, where did you get them?" WHY could you possibly want to know this? Are you a cross-dresser? Do you plan to go buy those $200 shoes for your sister's next birthday? It's obviously just a pointless, BORING question that says nothing about you and makes you look like a weasel. Another example is the infamous "Do you come here often?" What does it matter if she's there every week or just once a year? It's pointless so it flops.

So what makes for an original opener? Anything humorous, off-the wall, DIFFERENT. Something not too cheesy. Something that signals interest but also shows a little cockiness. Something that engages her interests and gets her wanting to open a discussion with you. Most importantly, something that DOESN'T suggest that you're all ga-ga over her, like "You're the most beautiful woman I've ever seen" or "Wow, you're so hot" (these openers give HER too much power and set the wrong tone for the interaction). The more of these factors you can combine into your opener, the better.

Feel free to come up with your own openers using the above criteria, or for fitting certain situations. Here are a few I've come up with or come across that do a good job of standing out and getting attention from your target:

Flattering Openers

Flattering openers are generally not a good idea, but they can be useful in certain situations. NEVER compliment a 9 or 10. She gets them ALL the time, and by NOT giving them, the girl will feel the LACK of attention (a self-esteem thing) and she will do things to TRY to elicit a favourable response from you (which means she is now chasing YOU).

"You're kinda cute"

"Is it hot in/out here or is it just you?"

"You're so sexy they should rename you DAMN." "You'd look good on my arm."

"I like your (hair, watch, etc). (Thanks). I like your   also. (Thanks). Come to think about it, I like a lot about you! What's your name?"

"If I looked as good as you, I'd stand in front of the mirror asking myself out all day. But I'd play hard to get since I don't want to be considered too easy..."

"What are you doing here? If I looked as good as you I'd be out in some bar getting free drinks all night!"

"Where's your paper bag?" (What??) "Your paper bag to put over your head. It's dangerous for someone like you to be out in public with all these horny people around. Don't worry, I'LL protect you!" (put arm around her protectively)

You see a good-looking girl walking down the street from a distance. Work it out so you accidentally get right in front of her and you both have to come to a screeching halt. Then, when she says, "Excuse me," or whatever, you say, "Oh, it's no problem. You would have stopped me in my tracks even if you weren't blocking my way!" For that head-on "weaving move" where people get confused and can't get around each other: "Hey thanks for the dance!"

"You look like a classy girl...Are you friendly?"

Full Guide to Being Cocky and Funny

Cocky & Funny Approaches

After eye contact/AI:

"Don't just look at me and keep walking! I'm not just a piece of meat you know! I have feelings too! Stop and talk to me…"
"Don't waste all that good eye contact! Stop and talk to me."

(you say Hi, she says Hi back but keeps moving) "Don't let a friendly HI go to waste! Stop and talk to me."

"Shall we talk or continue flirting from a distance?"

(Catching her looking) "Hi, I just couldn't help noticing you…(pause)… STARING at me!" (let sink in) "Do you always maintain such strong eye contact? Or only with guys like me that you can't help it with?"

Women's weird styles are easy targets for cocky & funny openers/comments. For slit skirts or pants:

"You POOR THING! Your pants/skirt is all ripped up the side/back!! You look like you were attacked by a Yorkie! Come on, we gotta get you new clothes!" (grab arm) "The Salvation Army is this way…" (Acting bitchy?) "Or maybe you need a rabies shot! Look how mean you're getting!" (denies) "Ok, well if I see you start foaming at the mouth I'm calling an ambulance".

"I'll bet you only shaved one leg to wear that skirt…or did you shave both legs? Prove it! Is your other leg as sexy as this one?" (Get her to let you feel/caress other leg to make sure it's shaved)

Full Guide to Being Cocky and Funny

For one-sided tank tops or one-sided long-sleeve tops:

"You POOR THING! You're too poor to afford the FULL shirt! Do you want a dollar or something? We gotta get you a real shirt! Come on I'm taking you shopping at Wal-Mart" (grab arm)

For one-sided long-sleeve tops:

"Oh my God! Your shirt is missing a sleeve. It looks like you were taken down by a police dog!"

For Von Dutch-style trucker caps:

"Hey, I like your hat...Let me guess, you're a long-haul trucker."

For shoes:

"Those are some pretty tall shoes. You must be like what, 4 foot 7 without them?"

"Hey, those are nice shoes. (pause) Some homeless kid must be running around barefoot right now!"

For animal print clothes:

"Hey, do you know how many (leopards/tigers/etc) had to die for that (shirt/skirt/etc)?? The animal rights people will have your ass."

Full Guide to Being Cocky and Funny

For a woman wearing leather skirt or high boots:

"You're wearing a leather skirt/boots! Some POOR cow had to die so you could show off your legs!"

For accessories:

"Those are some pretty earrings. I didn't know toy stores sold earrings like that!"

"What a cute ring (or watch or whatever)! Did you get that with the kids meal at McDonalds?"

"Wow, that's a huge purse. You don't have some little dog named Precious in there, do you?"

"So what's with the big purse, are you carrying a gun in there?"

(After labor day, and she's wearing white) "Hey, you're not supposed to wear white after Labor Day! I'm gonna call the fashion police on you! What's your name, I'm gonna report you right now." (if she resists) "Come on, what's your name? You can't run from the law, sooner or later they'll catch you." (later) Well you better go see the fashion police anyway, you know, do the right thing and turn yourself in. Just don't show up in bell-bottoms, you'll get more charges laid against you."

If she has a spot or stain on her clothes:

Point it out and say "What's the matter with you? Don't you know how to do laundry??"

For a woman with her roots showing:

Full Guide to Being Cocky and Funny

"Wow, how do you dye only the roots that dark color? That takes a lot of skill!"

For a general clothing opener (also gives you time to think of something about her clothing to bust on her about): Smile and say "Congratulations!" She'll say "For what?" Rip on her about her clothing, like "That's the skimpiest outfit I've seen all day" or "You make more noise walking in those shoes than anyone else".

Accusing her of common guy behavior is a great approach.

(Bumps into you) "Hey WHOA...hands off the merchandise!" (pause) "You know what, you're cute, I changed my mind...just don't touch the hot spots, OK? Try to control yourself until we get to know each other a little more".

(Bumps into you and says sorry) "It's ok. I know you were just trying to pick me up. You know, if you want to meet me all you have to do is say hi...you don't have to physically hit me." (haha) "I mean it, that's my WEAK arm you bumped into".

(Woman walking behind you) "Stop following me, I'm getting that stalker vibe from you!" (pause while she snaps out of her likely daydreaming) "And stop staring at my ass!" (I wasn't looking at your ass!) "Come on, I can feel your eyes burning a hole in the back of my pants! You can take a snapshot of it for $4.99...as long as it's for your personal enjoyment. Don't show it to all your friends."

(Woman walking behind you or standing behind you) "Hey are you staring at my ass??"

(Woman walking behind you) "Hey are you stalking me? I'm so tired of hot women following me around all day, it gets annoying."

Full Guide to Being Cocky and Funny

(she says Hey, I've seen you at   ) "Oh, so you were checking me out then?"

(If girl's been around a while) "Are you shy or something? Because I've been standing here for around ten minutes and you still haven't said Hi to me." (blah blah) "Every time I go some place women get all shy around me, since I'm such a good-looking, sexy man...As you can see."

C&F openers with push/pull:

"You're kinda CUTE...I think that you'll make a NICE new GIRLFRIEND! Hey WAIT...I need a girl who can cook...you can't?? OK, we're broken up... Actually wait, you DO smell good...very alluring...actually WAIT!! I'm allergic to that perfume...Oh man, we are SOOOO broken up!"

(In line at fast-food restaurant) "Damn...I-AM-SICK of this fast food...do you know how to cook? No?? Ok we're broken up then, I'm going to find a woman who can cook..." (while she cracks up, talk to another chick, then come back) "OK, so you can't cook... well, what else do you have going for you??? Are you adventurous?"

"You look familiar...I know! You look like my FUTURE ex-girlfriend!" Then follow up with a push-pull routine about how she could never by your future ex girlfriend because...but maybe you'll change your mind because...etc...

Specific street openers:

"Hey, are you good at accepting compliments from complete strangers?" (yeah) "Sweet, me too. You go first, compliment me."

Go up to a girl, start walking next to her, and say "Have you ever walked with a more sexy man?" OR "Does it upset you to be walking with such a sexy man because nobody's looking at you and everyone's looking at me?"

Full Guide to Being Cocky and Funny

"Look at this! When you woke up this morning did you ever think you'd be walking beside/talking to such a HANDSOME man, right here on (X) street? Your day just got a lot better!"

(In rain, walk up next to her and put umbrella over both of you) "Here, have some coverage. Hey, I just saved your bad hair day from getting worse, you owe me! Give me your number." (If she balks or gives attitude—odds are she won't give it to you so quickly—pull the umbrella away from her teasingly)

"Aww look at you, getting all wet again! I've got the umbrella, I'm the one wearing the pants in this relationship! Be nice to me."

In rain, walking past her: "Here, have some coverage..." (walk faster than her so you start passing her by) "Aww look, you walk too slow, and now you're getting rained on again!"

"Hey, where do you think you're going?" (to X) "Is THAT where you're going? You have to have greater goals in life!"

Girl ignores your opener and keeps walking: "What, did my good looks really scare you away that badly?"

"I bet you think you're hot shit." (for the really hard-ass/hot bitches who ignore you)

A couple general C&F openers:

"I realize you're probably shy because you get no attention from men whatsoever, so I decided to come over and pay attention to you"

Full Guide to Being Cocky and Funny

"You're KINDA hot. Are you friendly?" "Hey, you're kinda cute for a short girl"

C&F openers for specific situations:

(Eating ice cream or junk food) "You really shouldn't be eating that crap! You'll ruin your girlish figure." (blah blah) "FROZEN YOGURT is a healthy alternative. You should be eating frozen yogurt instead...With ME."

(Girl checking makeup in the mirror) "Don't worry, it doesn't look THAT bad!"

Girl checking her cell: "Did he call yet?"

(Supermarket opener) "Hi, you're cuter than the average woman I see in the (frozen foods/breakfast cereals) section...Are you friendly?"

Tyler Durden's Shopping/mall opener, Cliff's List: Grab a stupid jacket off the rack, and say "Whoa, this is SWEET...I should try this on NOW...come on, check this out." Then start moving to the mirror, and hopefully she'll start to come. Then GRAB BACK another jacket, the SAME ONE that you have. So now you BOTH try on the stupid jacket, and look in the mirror as you both look THE SAME. Put your arm around her like it's for a silly-picture, and look in the mirror together (role-playing couple). Then say "We should STEAL THESE", and watch her reaction, as you either playfully go along plotting how to do it, or she says NO. If she says "no", then GRAB HER STUFF, and PRETEND like you're running out the door with it. She'll tackle you, and then you say, "Know what?? I know a better way to make $$$. I need a RICH girl. Are you rich?" and start

QUALIFYING HER.

(GYM) "Can I ask you something?" This will get the head phones off... "How is this butt-firming machine working for you?" (Even though it's obvious to you how it's working, it's still a great opener) Then, after 2 minutes of talk, say "Thanks, I'm going to get back to my workout." Finally, before you leave, walk back over to her and contact-close.

(Sitting in some fast food place and she's about to walk by) Move out a chair with your foot, and say to the girl "There's a free chair here for you" She's resistant and asks "Oh really? Why should I sit there?" Nonchalantly reply "Well, I don't just want to get your number, I want to talk to you first."

(In a clothing store, sales girl walks up and says "Can I help you?") "Wow, this new cologne must be working... Every time I walk into a store a woman comes up to me and says Hi." (waiting for the subway, she's standing on the platform) "Don't fall onto the tracks! You'll make me late for work."

CELLULAR approach (street or terrasse) You look her in the eyes and say to your fictitious friend "Yeah, it's always the same story, girls keep ogling me...yeah...there's one in front of me, and you know what the worst is? She's shy...Yeah she's shy. She's been looking at me for X min. And she hasn't even started a conversation yet!...Ok...I mean, at least I appreciate the fact that she has a LOT of self-control; she hasn't felt me up so far." If she doesn't laugh HERE, well damn.

Girl walking her dog:

"Your dog is sooo cute!! What's the bitch's name?"

"Your dog is sooo cute!! What's his name?" (stop and check underneath dog) "Uhhhh, yeah. HIS name" or if it's a female, "Uhhhh, I mean HER name"

If you see her saying "Hi" to 1 or 2 guys she knows, open with "You're SUCH a player! Look at all the guys you know!"

Full Guide to Being Cocky and Funny

She's standing behind you. Look over your shoulder: "You're trouble". (I'm not trouble) "YES you are! You look like a total bad girl! You just got out of jail, didn't you?"

She's digging through her purse: "It looks like you're trying to steal from that purse. I'll have to have you arrested/thrown out of the club."

Woman appears melancholy or depressed: Say "Sucks to be you" and wink at her. (What? Why??) Laugh and say "You look like you just lost your best friend".

Girl getting unwanted attention from obvious jerks: Roll up and link arms with her so you're in between. "We were just going to X, right?" (yeah let's go). While walking away: "You have some creepy friends".

You're standing behind a girl who's reading a newspaper or magazine. Read it over her shoulder, and as soon as she turns the page say "Hey wait, I'm not done reading that yet!" If she apologizes say "I forgive you." Wait a second then say "OKAY, you can turn the page now." Say "Do you always re ad magazines/crap newspapers like this? You seemed a lot more intellectual than that..."

Sexual Innuendo C&F Approaches

Generally it's not a good idea to make a sexually suggestive comment when opening. When you see a hot woman, put that lust away so you can enjoy it later—with her! But there may be situations where such an opener is appropriate, like if the girl seems the type, you've had prior friendly contact with her, etc.

"That's a great outfit you're ALMOST wearing" (Strip club or bar or general) ELEVATOR: "You know, if this elevator gets stuck, we could be trapped in here for weeks. And then I'd have to EAT you..."

"In my next life I want to come back as those pants!"

Full Guide to Being Cocky and Funny

Humorous Approaches

"Hi, do you know any good opening lines?"

PEZ OPENER: You walk up to a girl, tilt your head to the side and look serious, stare for a second and wait for her to give you the "What do you want" look. Crack a half smile, and pull out the Pez. "Pez?" (girl takes it) "Didn't your mom warn you about taking candy from strangers?" (Yeah...) "And it's bad for your teeth."

"You look like the kind of girl I'd want backing me up in a bar fight"

(Sabastian's dept store pickup, Cliff's List) We were in some lame ass store. I was walking around with bra on its hanger hanging from my shirt collar and a pair of matching panties hanging from my belt. This time I accosted the test subject. I could tell by her Abercrombie look that I would have to come in as just a jerk and work my way up to total fucking dickhead asshole. Sabastian: "How do I look?" Katie: What? Oh um, I don't know. Sabastian: "C'mon, tell me what you think, I don't have all day. Think I have a shot at being a Victoria's Secret model?"

Shopping in office supplies: "Could I have your opinion? Which pen looks better? This one (hold it up beside face in James Bond pose like with a gun) or this BiC?" (cross arm and hold pen up by face with model pose)..."How about you just write your number here so I can see how sexy it looks while you're writing..."

Standard Approaches

STORE: "Excuse me... what do you think?" and put on/hold up whatever you're considering. "Would you buy these if you were me?"

Full Guide to Being Cocky and Funny

(Elvis opener) "Hey, did you know that Elvis dyed his hair? He was naturally BLOND, but he thought black hair made him more striking." (blah blah) "What freaks me out about Elvis was the way the girls used to scream and cry at his concerts, they used to drown him out. You don't see that today-- maybe women are more jaded. Did you find Elvis hot? Would YOU be one of the chicks screaming at him??" (blah blah) "Young Elvis or OLD Elvis?" (blah blah) "Yeah, old Elvis was kinda scary. What singer do you find REALLY sexy today?"

Opinion Openers

Opinion openers are generally "safe". They're indirect, and you're not putting the woman on the spot to accept or reject you. They can be used on single targets, or group sets (including group sets that include guys). If someone has low confidence or doesn't like the C&F approach, this is a safe way to go. They're just ways to start up a conversation. If you're approaching a group of girls with an opinion opener, don't say "Hi ladies" or "Hi girls", which only sets the approach up as a man approaching a woman, with all its social boundaries. You want to get into the group as "one of the guys", so say "Hey guys!" Once you're in conversation, THEN you can pull out the cocky & funny comments, tease her, etc.

FALSE TIME CONSTRAINTS are very effective when using opinion openers. Keep in mind that if you approach someone she may be thinking about something, not want to be approached, be on her way somewhere, etc. If you say "Hey I only have a minute but I want to get a female opinion on something", you give her the impression that the interaction won't take too long and she'll be less likely to blow you off because of her obligations. And if you happen to end up talking to her for half an hour, it doesn't make you a liar. In her mind it means that you were only intending to talk for a minute or two, but you guys hit it off so well that it "just happened" like that. A well-executed contact- close should only take a couple minutes anyway, so you're not necessarily being dishonest.

"Hey do girls really think that Colin Farrell is hot?" (better than "hi", because she actually ENJOYS giving her opinion on stupid shit like this) "See, the way I see it is that Brad Pitt's getting a little old to be a fantasy boytoy. So Colin Farrell's being groomed to be the new Brad Pitt. Who do girls think is hotter, Colin Farrell or Brad Pitt?" If they like Brad Pitt, say "Well the guy's like 40 years old! That's OLD!!! Are you saying you guys like OLD MEN?"

"Hey, my friend and I were having a discussion today and I need a female opinion. Who do you think lies more, men or women? See, I think that women lie more than men, but men are just worse at HIDING that they're lying." (blah blah blah) "Women are people-pleasers, they don't like to hurt people's feelings. So they lie all the time to avoid giving people the ugly truth, and it becomes almost AUTOMATIC for them. Sometimes they don't even realize they're doing it." (blah blah blah). Whatever she answers, accuse her of lying about her answer/opinion! "Now see, THAT sounds totally made up. THAT sounds like a lie!" And later, when you contact close you can use call-back humor and playfully ask "Is this your REAL number, or are you LYING?" Or if she says she has a boyfriend when you go to contact-close, say "Do you REALLY have a boyfriend or are you LYING?"

Hey I can't stick around long, but I NEED a female opinion on something: Ok, one of my friends broke up with his girlfriend 3 months ago. They were together for 2 years, but he felt it was time to go. Now the thing is, even though they were broken up, they were still doing everything they used to do together. They hung out a lot, went out together, hung around with the family, they even still slept together. Now just this week the guy went on a date with another girl, and he ended up sleeping with her. His ex-girl heard about it and now she's EXTREMELY pissed!! Now, my question is: Do you think she has a right to be mad, since technically they were broken up?" (blah blah blah) "Well what if he thought that SHE'D slept with someone else?" (blah blah blah) "Have you ever been in a similar situation?"

Dental floss opener: "I need your opinion on something/settle something for us: Are you supposed to floss BEFORE or AFTER brushing your teeth?"

The hair colour change opener: "What would you think if I dyed my hair completely BLACK?" (blah blah) "What about blond with black highlights?" (blah blah) "Ok then... how about I keep my hair blond....but with BLACK ROOTS?" (blah blah) "Did you know Elvis was blond, but he dyed his hair black?"

Full Guide to Being Cocky and Funny

Bars/Clubs Openers

In a club, in the typical frame the woman has all the sexual power. Even the ugliest girl still has more sexual power than the hottest guy there, since there will always be some guy there with enough booze in him to sleep with her. So you REALLY have to set yourself apart and show her that she has no sexual power over you. In clubs you have to open with strong statements. Because there's so much competition, and the women have so much power in the situation, everything in the beginning has to be nothing but VALUE, VALUE, VALUE or you won't get in to the set and stay in. Boldness, C&F, humour, they all count. Once you're in the door, it's action-action-action and worshipping the 3-seconds rule. Or you can dance near the edge of the dance-floor and pull any girls passing by to dance with you. Or you can act like you already know the girl, take her hand, nod towards the dance floor and say "Well, come on!". If she seems reluctant, you go "Oh, come on!". If she says "I'm tired", BOOM, you're in a conversation! "Tired? Well, not that you mention it, this place is a little crowded/noisy. Why don't we go to someplace quieter where we can talk and you can relax" If you let go of her hand in the meantime, grab it again and guide her to a nice and quiet little corner you've already checked out before.

On kiss closes: (Tyler Durden, Cliff's List)

DO NOT kiss-close in clubs, unless you have MAD rapport first. REFUSE all kiss- closes. Holding out and building massive rapport, or using time-distortion, is key to showing her that "this is not just a club fling". If she's all over you: "Hands off the merchandise!" If you find yourself kissing her, it's important that YOU be the one to end it first, pulling back and saying something like "Ohhhhh man this is going too fast, we need to control ourselves, etc." The reason for this is that women LOVE foreplay. While guys go out hoping to get sex, a woman can just go out week after week and kiss and grope guys in clubs, and still be satisfied. If you want to see her beyond the club, including taking her home that same night, you have to demonstrate massive value and rapport, and show that you're not just some "One-Night-Foreplay-Stand". Show her that you can control yourself, and you're hard-to-get.

STANDING NEXT TO HB IN BAR: "Will you PLEASE stop touching me?" (Oh, I'm sorry… I didn't know that I was touching you) "Well, you did. And if you're gonna keep doing it, I'd appreciate it if you'd touch a little higher." (Well, touchy touchy) "Don't make me get a chaperone."

(On dance floor or in line at the bar) "Hey, did you just touch my ass?" (no) "No? Well you should!" If the girl finds you cute and feels safe (or tipsy), and she's in a fun mood, she may even slap or touch your ass at that point. Act shocked and say "I was only kidding! I feel VIOLATED. I need a shower now! Or a drink. Buy me a drink."

"What are you doing at a bar? Can't you find a nice normal guy? Or are you desperate?"

If she asks for a light:

(do you have a light?) "Yeah" (pull out, light it, then pull it back) "You know, smoking's really bad for you! It's a dangerous habit." (blah blah) "So, do you have any other dangerous habits?" (suggestively, while lighting cig, her: blah blah) "Like approaching strangers and asking for a light?"

(do you have a light?) "Well it depends. Do you want it to light a cigarette or start a fire in the club?"

You should ALWAYS carry a lighter when you go to a club or bar, since if you don't have one, the woman will ask another guy and engage HIM in conversation instead. If you're peacocking with a cool, interesting lighter (and you SHOULD be) she may make a favorable comment on it (Oh, that lighter's so cool!/Nice lighter!/Let me see it!/etc), say C&F: "You don't care about me, you're just interested in my lighter! How about I leave my lighter with you so that you two can have a nice conversation?"

Or if you're talking to a woman at a bar, and the conversation is going well, you say

Full Guide to Being Cocky and Funny

"OK, let's just cut to the chase... are you going to offer to buy me a drink or what?"

IF SHE SNUBS A DANCE: "Ok, if you want to dance with me later, I'll be around. If I don't have another good-looking girl on my arm then ask me to dance."

CLUBBING METHOD #1 (Cliff's List, unknown author)

1.   First I believe you should approach clubbing like a military operation. That is, run it like a business.

2.   Avoid hanging with your friends in the club, UNLESS they are extremely good at getting women.

3.   Once at the club. Avoid the girls with the big purse/hand bag, like the plague. Do they-date, fuck, have relationships, needs love too? Yes, certainly. However, based on my observation, they are usually the designated drivers, baby sitters (friend sitter), for the night.

4.   Similarly, at parties avoid the young ladies whom you see with condoms, pinned to their outfit. The condoms mean they want to get all the guys' attention, not that they want to bang.

5.   Always be having fun, no matter what. Even if you are out there on the dance floor alone, act like you are having more fun than any one in the room. Just be having what I call "crazy fun." Hi-five everyone (both male and female) on or around the dance floor, even if you have never seen them before in your life. Continue saying, "hi" to everyone and his/her dog in the club and having fun.

6.   I never, ever (at least no longer, I should say) ask, "do you have a boyfriend?" Why? I have found that most (many) women will fuck your brains out when she is in the mood, despite having a boyfriend.

Full Guide to Being Cocky and Funny

7.   Never hold up the wall. Have you ever noticed that there is very little space at the walls? The guys who hold up the wall and still get laid are usually the sport players (basketball, football, etc.) Women usually come to those guys. Get yourself in the middle of the dance floor or somewhere speaking with girls or just simply go home. Avoid being one of the losers on "DEATH ROW".

8.   I usually go on the dance floor as soon as I enter the club(s), even if it's empty. Why? Well, ironically because I am not the best dancer in the world. Thus, while many guys need a few beers before hitting the dance floor, I just go out there and start moving. Yes, I view it as warming up.

9.   Now, I do believe eye contact and all that is important. However, I never, ever just wait for it in the club. Instead, I simply walk up to a girl or groups of girls (group of one to ten or more.) Then with the biggest smile on my face, I hug them/her and say, "hi". Note carefully: I always hug or put my arms around her/them in one form or another, when I approach. That is, whether I approach from behind, the side or front, I place my arms on them while smiling and saying, "that was so cool/funny," etc.

10.   Know your audiences, the approach that works on Jen, may or may not work on April or Allison. Greet her, move away, and return later. She will determine if she wants you to stick around like an appendage.

11.   Now this is a very big one, guys. If you take nothing else, this is the biggest secret for you. If a girl refuses your approach early in the night, it does not mean go away and never return. Never ask why she does not want to dance. She has every right to refuse. Which, most of the times has nothing in the world to do with you. So just go away. However, with that same big smile, just say, "[*her name], I will speak with you later on" and keep smiling on leave. Now keep dancing and have "mad-crazy fun." Dance and make out with other young ladies. Then later on say, "hi" to the young lady/ladies who refuse before. Depending on how they had said, "no" the first time will gauge the way you approach the second time around. However, always, always give every woman at least a second chance to get to know you. Often

she usually doesn't remember turning you down before.

12.   Don't be afraid to be seen making out. Women don't mind, in fact, they seem to love seeing you making out with other women in the club. It gets easier to pick up the next girl and the next group in the club when you are already making out with other women. It seems like women only want what other women have. I have had women say "you were the guy over there making out with my friend Kim." Yet, within 5 minutes we are at it.

13.   Now how do I know that she wants to make out? Do I ask her? NO! I have noticed that when a girl wants you to kiss her. She will start to give you this incredible eye scan and they almost always part their lips. They have that luscious look to their lips. That is, their lips are not pursed together instead it's parted and she is licking them. When I just started out girls use to ask, "are you just shy, why don't you kiss me?" Now I just watch for the above signs. Then I simply brush back her hair (as she smiles) and hold her face in my left hand and plant one on her. Then I pull back slightly.

14.   Don't ever get drunk and finally, never, ever go home with a drunken girl (possible rape charge if she has misgivings later on).

CLUBBING METHOD #2

The connection game (Cliff's List, unknown author)

Uses social proof created from scratch in the venue. Chat some girls up for literally 2 minutes, then tell them "Hold on a minute, I have to say hi to someone." Walk over to some other girls you don't know at all and do the same thing. The concept is simple, just hold their interest, be funny, and leave first. And leave to talk to another girl, make it clear you are going to another girl.

Why? This makes them jealous, you didn't have time to fuck up, and they will look for you later, especially after all of the social proof you get through this method.

Full Guide to Being Cocky and Funny

Because you end up appearing to know everyone. Once one of the girls says hi to you later, you know you can have her. It's really that simple. This works wonders compared to the slow process of entertaining girls.

<I'll use an example that really exemplifies his style so you can get the idea. Natural and I go to a club downtown on a Thursday. Right after entering he spots a girl he already knows. We walk over to her and he says hi to her. She's with a gorgeous friend who he doesn't even talk to, and he stops me from talking to her. We chat up his friend until she introduces us, maybe 3 minutes. Then all he says to the hottie is "hey" then talks to his friend some more. This is where the game begins. He turns to the hot girl right when it looks like she's getting bored, "Where are you from?" Dumb question right? Who gives a shit, she was bored, she wanted attention. She's from such and such a city. "Oh, you're one of THOSE kind of girls?" ("What kind of girls?") My friend then looks, smiles, begins to answer then cuts himself off. "I need to go say hi to a friend I'll be back." Off we go to a two set sitting down. He carries over his drink. "I can't stand when I drink, it makes me tired. So you guys get my attention until I finish this drink. (It's almost finished) You guys look like best friends?" They laugh, talk for a bit, just natural convo, but before it gets boring, and before he finishes his drink- up and away- same line: "I need to go say hi to a friend." Cut through a lot of talking and fun times meeting people, we now know basically every girl in the club. Girls do come and say hi but not the ones we want. So we walk by them talking to other girls. Here's the funny maneuver that I didn't explain. When he wants to re-get the attention of a hottie, he says "Hey, don't I know you from somewhere? You seem so familiar, and for the first time this isn't a pick up line." They laugh and say we met earlier. One is this big-titted girl, the other is this small petite 8. He chats with them, I talk to their guy friend to keep him busy. Natural comes to me and says ok we're going to their place. I assume he closed the way he usually does. "This club is closing and I'm not even tired yet, lets keep the party going, and get drunk back at your place." He comes off non-threatening, and genuine about still partying. and it works for him. We get to their place. Lots of people are over, drugs are everywhere. People are doing lines right and left. I get offered a variety of supplements, but I wanted to keep my head straight. Natural grabs me and tells me to sit on the couch next to Big tittie HB, but don't talk to her, talk to everyone else, and pretend like she's not there, until she starts talking to me directly, then pull her to the table away from everyone else. I do this and it works. We then talk and build rapport for a good 6 hours, it's 8 in the morning or so, we go back to her room and do the good deed. Tuesday night is 80's night at one of the

clubs in town here. Natural called me up and told me to meet him there. We get inside the club, sure enough he knows some girls, and he strikes up conversation with them. "Shit, we just got here and I promised I'd get my friend plastered, so we have to get going." He ejects quickly and we go upstairs in the club and bump into a girl he helped me work last time. 3 guys were hitting on her so we chilled with the guys and ignored her. She comes and says hi to us. He tells me to kiss her and then walk away from her telling her I'm busy. I do it. On the line to the girls' bathroom there are a group of hotties he doesn't know. I try to open them, I forgot what I said, but it was a bad opener. He jumps in "my friend is drunk right now, you know how it is." Have you ever been to Mexico? Yeah you have. Well, you know how they have guys there who just come up to you and sell you things, but of course they turn out to be the federali?" He cuts her off "Oh I gotta say hi to a friend, hold that thought.">

6. Opening Groupsets

Groups of around 5 girls are fairly easy to approach. You don't have to entertain them ALL (this is valid if they're not all talking about the same thing but are rather segmented). Instead pick ONE of them (most of the time it's the one who seems the most bored) and just start to chat it up. RARELY will the other girls try to pull the girl away. Instead, it brings out the competitive spirit in the other girls and then THEY will be the ones breaking YOUR conversation, and not the other way around. Now the girl you approach might not be very interested in you but as long as you look like your having a good time and your not getting completely blown off, stay with it. IF THERE'S A GIRL IN THE GROUP WHO FINDS YOU ATTRACTIVE SHE'LL MAKE HERSELF KNOWN. She'll either give you very strong eye contact, or she'll try to join into the conversation or she'll approach you.

Mystery Method approach to groupsets

Mystery's method springs from his theory that a true 10 can't be approached directly. She will require a prospective suitor to achieve social validation and proof prior to admission to her exclusive and wonderful world. Thus, Mystery's students are instructed to tackle two-sets and three sets around the ultimate target, to parlay the conquests and parade the pawns around the room as clear demonstrations of desirability and worth prior to putting any moves on Miss Magnificence herself. According to Mystery, scoring a 10 (the only type of babe Mystery plays for) is a matter of making many chess-like moves on the high- stakes playing-field that the ignorant refer to as a bar, a party, or a club. He says any man can do it, but you gotta play the game to win.

A 10 is almost never alone. By virtue of her beauty other women or men will be hanging around her. So when approaching the target, the key is to befriend the group, to disarm the OBSTACLES. When the vibe is good and you've gotten EVERYONE laughing, THEN you pay attention to the one you want. Pay attention to the ugly girls first. By paying more attention to them first, you make them like you as a person and at the same time the pretty TARGET feels a bit self-conscious that she 't getting the attention she usually gets. Only when everyone likes you do you FINALLY give the TARGET the attention she now craves. When you notice you are paying a bit too much attention to her, that's when you ask for permission from your new friends to isolate her: "This girl's cool, I'm just gonna STEAL her away from you guys for a sec." When isolated, tell her "Look at what you made me do. I had to make EVERYONE here like me before I could talk to you. See that? This would have been so much easier if you were alone."

In some cases, it may be better to go straight to the target rather than engaging the whole group. Do what's natural, and follow the path of least resistance in the particular situation.

Groupset Approaches

Groups are usually easier to approach from a rejection standpoint. Since one woman can't read her friends' minds, she won't tell you they're not interested. After all, maybe her friend(s) really like you and actually want to keep you around. Also, the "safety-in-numbers" aspect works in your favor. You'll be seen as less threatening than if you'd approached one of them alone.

False time-constraining is important when opening groups. In most cases you'll be interrupting a conversation, so you have to make it look as if you're only a temporary, inoffensive intrusion. "Hey guys, I only have a minute but I wanted a female opinion on something..." Stand sideways as you open them so that they feel less threatened.

After you get past the first opener, you should take a seat with them while going into the second one. Definitely take a seat; if you just stand there you risk looking stupid. If it comes down to it, grab a chair from another table and bring it over as you do your first opener.

"You guys are gonna turn a lotta heads tonight. What club are you going to?" (answer) "Aww come on...go to a REAL club! You guys are way too good for that place!" OR "You have great taste in fashion but lousy taste in clubs!" OR "You can't go there, you'll make the other women look bad."

(If they're all wearing similar clothes/style) "Aww isn't that cute. You're all dressed alike! You look like the Power Puff Girls or something!"

Groupset Opinion Openers:

"Hey Guys, I can't stick around long, but I NEED a female opinion on something: Ok, one of my friends broke up with his girlfriend 3 months ago. They were together for 2 years, but he felt it was time to go. Now the thing is, even though they were broken up, they were still doing everything they used to do together. They hung out a lot, went out together, hung around with the family, they even still slept together. Now just this week the guy went on a date with another girl, and he ended up sleeping with her. His ex-girl heard about it and now she's EXTREMELY pissed!! Now, my question is: Do you think she has a right to be mad, since technically they were broken up?" (If they accuse YOU of being the guy who did all this) "No way! If it was ME then there'd be two supermodels involved and a lot of leather!"

An example of a simple 2-on-2 approach : "Hi... my friend isn't from here (introduce friend)... so how do you guys know each other?" You can also use this to approach a larger group. "So how does everyone know everyone else?" That line is great...Especially when the truth comes out and the guy in the set that THOUGHT he was here on a date finds out he's only HANGING OUT with the girl he wants and she declares herself free for the taking.

(Available chair approach) Walk up to one or more women who are sitting at one of these outdoor cafe tables. Be sure you walk up to a group where there is a chair at their table that isn't being used. Maybe you should buy something at the cafe first, but that's probably not required. You then smile and say, "Hi, I was wondering if this chair was being used by anybody / I was wondering... can I take this chair?" They'll say no / yes, the chair's available. They assume you need to borrow it for some table you'll be eating at. So after they answer you, give a big cocky smile and sit yourself down in the chair. "Thanks! So how do you all know each other?" OR "Is this the singles' table? I need your opinions...what do women really want?" Usually they'll spout off some shit about caring, nurturing, blah blah, but brush it all off and say: "BORING...How about some HONEST answers now? None of you brought up anything SEXUAL...like a man who can last for 4 hours, sleep one hour, and then do it all over again! (sp) You all disappoint me!" Other opinion openers are perfect for groupsets as well.

"Hey, I have to leave in a minute but I need some female opinions. Who do you think lies more, men or women?" Then go into the Lies opinion opener.

"Hey I need a female opinion...wait, you're all FEMALE right? No cross- dressers here? Ok..." Then go into an opinion opener.

Once they get talking and giving their opinions, things will probably get animated and they'll all be talking over each other. Say "Oh my God, it's like the View here" It can last a good 15 minutes as they all chime in. If guys are there too you can say, "What the hell, let's get your opinion too."

Groupset Ejecting

"Well, you're all a very attractive group of ladies, but I can't stay long or the group of supermodels I'm with might get really pissed. Unless you're ready to fight for me!"

Full Guide to Being Cocky and Funny

If everybody is standing, suggest a GROUP HUG when you leave. If the interaction has gone well, just say "Group Hug!!" and start bringing everyone close together so you can hug them all at once.

7. Bitch Shield destroyers

The hotter the woman, the thicker the shell and the thicker the barrier you need to break down. Mystery came up with the concept of Negative Hits. "Neg Hits" serve to break down the "Bitch Shield". They provide a "lift" in the form of a compliment, then a "drop" in the form of a comment that COULD be taken negatively. Or the order could be reversed—Drop to lift. Don't insult her, but make sure she understands that you aren't going to smother her in praise just because she's an attractive woman. The best way to defeat the bitch shield is with a smile (and lots of eye contact). C&F openers tend to have a built-in Neg Hit effect, so additional Negs may not be needed—judge each situation on its own merits.

"Nice nails. are they real?" She will have to concede, "No, acrylic." and you say (like you didn't notice it was a put down) "Oh. (pause) Well I guess they still LOOK good." Then you turn your back to her.

"Wow, those are interesting shoes." She'll say, "Thanks!" And you say, "But I think you should get them in blue instead of black."

(acting bitchy) "What's wrong? Not used to talking to guys as devastatingly handsome as me? You wanna talk about it?"

"You drank too much last night didn't you? Your eyes look a little red. That's okay though, you still look pretty hot".

"Your nose wiggles when you speak. its sooo cute!"

Full Guide to Being Cocky and Funny

Take gum out and offer it to her. "No thanks I'm drinking beer." Reply, "I know... take the gum."

"I bet you're even prettier without so much make-up on."

"Your eyes are pretty red. You haven't been treating your body very well lately have you?"

"That's a nice dress." (Thanks) "I remember seeing you at a club before and you were wearing the same dress. It IS nice though."

"What do you do?" (Oh, I'm a model.) "Oh, that's cool. Like a hand model or something?"

"That's a cheesy   . Well, at least you're lucky to have a nice body." (to compensate for whatever it was you negged)

"You are nearly as tall as me. I like tall girls." (LIFT) "Are those heels 4 or 5 inches?" (DROP)

"You blink a lot"

"Weren't you wearing this dress the last time you were here?"

"Oh...You just spit on me." (when the girl is talking to you). "That's okay though, I don't mind women drooling all over me."

"Your hair looks nice. Is that your natural color?"

"I don't think we should get to know each other." (Why?) "I think you are just too much of a NICE GIRL for me." (whatever, it doesn't matter because she will try for you now)

"Just out of curiosity, am I too young for you?"

"Your perfume (or piece of clothing) doesn't suit you. You should be wearing something that brings out your youthful character."

"I guess you're trying to join the (insert celebrity name here) club when it comes to hairstyles. I've seen a lot of women with a similar style, but I must say it suits you a lot better than most women."

8. Boyfriend Destroyers

Don't ever, ever ask if she has a boyfriend! Maybe she does, maybe not. So what, who cares? Maybe she's with her bf for security and wants to have fun on the side. Maybe she's about to leave him. Most 9s and 10s are never single, they always find another guy before dropping the one they have.

(I have a boyfriend) "Good! It will give you something to do when I'm not around."

(I have a boyfriend) "How many boyfriends do you have?" (Just one) "Just one? I think you should have at least 2"

(I have a boyfriend) "*Laughing* Hey, I just met you and you're already telling me your problems?"

"I think we should get together and do X on Xday." (I have a boyfriend) "Okay so

Xday at 8 it is! Dress sexy."

(I have a boyfriend) "Well I'm not inviting HIM, just YOU."

(I have a boyfriend) "So when's the wedding? I mean, since he's meeting EVERY DESIRE you have, exactly the way YOU NEED IT FULFILLED, you must be planning on marriage, right? That way you can spend the REST OF YOUR LIFE, just with him, forever and ever and ever. That's so sweet!"

(I have a boyfriend) "Well, we're gonna have to be really careful when we sneak around then" (Sorry, I can't. NOT gonna happen) "Of course not! I was just testing you. So let's see, how about this Saturday evening? Tell him you have to meet the girls for a Tupperware party or something and sneak over to my house." (No way) "Of course not! How could you ever live with yourself? Ok, I'll put the champagne on ice around 7, so if you get to my house by around 8, it should be perfect."

(I have a boyfriend) "Great! I have a girlfriend. So your boyfriend won't mind. Just two friends getting together!" (You have a girlfriend? What's your girlfriend's name?) "What day is it today?" (Xday) "Well then, my girlfriend's name is Maria..."

9. Objections Destroyers

You're too old/How old are you? "I'm 29 years YOUNG. But from the waist down I'm still 18" OR "Young enough to put my arm around you without people whispering" (Put arm around her) "See? No one's saying 'Hey look at that young girl and that geezer together!'" OR "Old enough that if you do something with me you won't go to jail!" OR (serious) "Do you wanna keep dating college boys, or do you want to date someone... (pause)...who knows what he's doing?" (sp) OR "Old enough to buy beer. Want me to buy you some so you don't have to pull out that fake ID?"

How old are you? "Why, do you want to brag to all your friends about how you met this gorgeous older guy?"

Full Guide to Being Cocky and Funny

How old are you? Scowl at her and ask "How much do you weigh?"

You're too young! "I have a very bright future, and I like older women."

I don't like blond guys! "But everybody knows blonds have more fun! You like to have fun don't you?"

I don't have time for this! "Whatever it is, I'm WORTH being late for it!"

I'm not interested! "Why, are you intimidated by my STUNNING good looks? Or is it my arrogant charm?" OR "After 2 minutes of knowing me you'll be VERY interested"

I don't like muscular guys! "I'm not muscular, I just carry my fat well"

I don't like skinny guys! "I'm not skinny, I just wear skinny clothes"

I'm too busy for another guy in my life right now! "Ok then...I guess you'll have to DITCH one of the others so you'll have time for ME!"

You're a stranger, I don't talk to strangers! "Hey that's HANDSOME stranger to you!" (playing hard to get or ignoring you) "Oh, I get it...You wanna be CHASED!" OR "Playing hard-to-get already? But we just met, don't start playing games until later!"

10. Specific Circumstances Openers

A Girl You Already Know

Let's say you see a girl you know, but who may or may not know you. Like maybe a girl you've seen in a college class or from work. You want to stick to your game plan like she's any other girl until she recalls that she knows you. For instance, you don't want to go up to her and tell her "Hey! I saw you at the company picnic last summer!" or something like that. You want to let HER initiate that kind of connection, because if she doesn't remember you (or she does and you bring up where you know her first), she has the power in the interaction.

The same thing is true for a set you've already opened and see later on. If you've already opened them, don't go up and say "Hey, remember me?" Just stick to your plan. If they remember you, they'll bring it up.

Internet Openers

General

Most of the principles outlined above apply to internet Find/Open as well. Still, here are some guidelines and just plain "lines" that are suited for picking up on the net:

1) Watch the personals every day. Only send messages to the NEW ads. If a woman's been on the network for more than a couple weeks, she's probably bitter and skeptical about Internet dating. There are a LOT of freaks on those dating networks.

2) When you get a reply, email and ask her for her number. Tell her that you're swamped with a million messages from supermodels who keep bragging about how much money they have, and she needs to act fast or you'll be gone.

3) Get her number as soon as possible, and get her ON THE PHONE. This is the goal, don't waste weeks chatting and chatting (you risk STALING out the girl). "Okay this chatting thing is fun but let's talk on the phone now like NORMAL people. Unless you want to stay Internet pen pals forever LOL" Give her your number, and as soon as you hit ENTER, type "I don't hear my phone ringing" :op

4) DO NOT, under ANY circumstances talk about lame NORMAL stuff.

C&F example of a good first message to send: "Wow….from your profile you sound like an interesting, intelligent, balanced woman. Are you SURE you're from this planet?? lol I'm usually pretty busy rejecting marriage offers from rich supermodels and volunteering with orphaned puppies, but I'm sure I could find some time to chat with you. ;o) I can be reached at (@youremail.com) Talk to me."

"Well, you seem really nice. I'd invite you to call me, but I'm afraid that you might be one of these weirdoes...or some guy pretending to be a woman..." (pause) "You know, coffee is a safe bet...This way if you're scary in person, I can say "Oh, hey... um... I just remembered that I have to go feed my parrot...It's really important..." and then we can call it a night."

If they don't answer emails or instant messages, don't get frustrated. She may have been busy answering someone else, or have been otherwise busy. Or she might be deliberately holding back from writing from you to see if you write an insecure "What's wrong? Don't you like me??" Instead, write back a little later: "What, playing hard to get already? Nice. Talk to me." This should get a response back if she's at all interested.

Internet first-chat fluff talk

"So what brought you to the net, (name)? Not meeting any quality guys (such as myself) in "real life"?"

"So have you met anyone interesting on the net yet? Aside from me I mean."

"Most women on the Internet need a spanking. Are you an Internet Diva?" (What do you mean?) "Well, some women on the net get really big egos from Internet dating. There are tons of loser guys emailing them every day, and they get this big attitude. The funny thing is, a lot of these Internet Divas are women most guys wouldn't look twice at on the street!" Later, whenever she cops an attitude you just say "Internet Diva!"

"You know what I don't like about online meeting? You know that connection you get with someone emotionally, like you've known them for years? You're talking or chatting with him and you think "I'm on the same level as this person, the same wavelength..." With me I find that all the time online." (her: blah blah) "But the "physical buzz", the chemistry, often that's not there when you meet." (pause/next IM) "You know when you meet a guy in real life, you see the looks first. When you get attracted to this guy the physical buzz comes first and the emotional connection comes a lot easier after that." (pause/next IM) "The Internet takes that process of NATURE, built into us over millenia, and turns it BASS-ACWARDS." (pause) "It's normal to see first and connect later. The internet doesn't allow that...That's why it usually feels weird when you meet, cuz it's unnatural." (push for "natural" meeting or call ASAP to see if the "physical buzz" is there "so we don't waste our time". Build a bit of rapport before doing this though since she won't meet you if you just started chatting 5 minutes ago).

(The stranger objection to meeting "I don't even know you!") "Yes you do! I'm an Internet chat program, Mike 6.0"

Online, call them BRAT as soon as reasonably possible. Tell her she has no life because she's chatting with men on the net.

If her responses take too long to come on an IM chat: "TYPE FASTER! Giddy up! Come on, Speedy!"

"You're really a man, aren't you?" "You're too old for me"

"You're not a bitch, you're a brat. Bitches need to be slapped, BRATS need to be spanked"

If there's a long pause between replies from her: "What are you up to? Are you chatting with someone else right now? I'm too busy for that, talk to you later." Then ignore her for 10 minutes. Come back and if she's sent something for you in the meantime, say "Oh, so I have all of your attention now?"

She asks how old you are: "I'm really 104 but I lie so hot women will want to chat with me"

One way to bring up the meeting topic: "It's TIME to meet". (rather than asking if she wants to meet—weak)

Waitress "takedowns"

A waitress is a captive audience. She has to be nice, or pretend to be. No bitch shield in sight. Go totally cocky/funny on waitresses!

(how many are in your group) "Three of us...FOUR if YOU join us..." "We want the good-looking section, please".

Full Guide to Being Cocky and Funny

(Are you ready to pay?) "See? All women want is my money...They're all a bunch of gold diggers!"

Waitress overcharges you by accident, go C&F: "You're trying to scam me aren't you? I'm not THAT blond/dumb! You thought you could pull a fast one on me, didn't you?" (says "sorry" for making a mistake or if a dish you want isn't available) "You're fired!"

If she lingers a little too long at your table talking: "You're never gonna make enough money to support me if you keep ignoring your other tables!"

At a bar: Start calling your waitress NURSE..."Oh, pain, bring me beer!" "Give me a shot to take away the pain" "Tuck me into my hospital bed"

Zan's Waitress Takedown Technique, Cliff's List

Her: What can I get for you?

You: "Hi, I haven't seen you around before. What's your name?"

Her: My name is Stephanie. What's yours?

You: "I'm Mike. And I'll have a (choose rare drink)." (big smile...If no rare drink, say) "Well there's a liquor store down the street, if you go and pick one up for me I'll give you a nice tip". (check pockets) "I think I have a dollar around here somewhere". When she's about to leave, say "Pleasure for you to meet me, Stephanie".

The next time she comes around:

You: "You again? Wow, you sure like to hang around us, don't you?"

Her: (laughs) (blah blah) You: (some other blah blah) Her: (some other blah)

You: (as she is leaving) "I have a feeling you'll come back to see us again real soon. You can't resist us!"

Her: (smiling) Yeah, I can't resist.

Of course, she has to come back to your table; she's the waitress! And when she does, smile at her and give the other guys a knowing look in front of her.

"See, I was right, she's back!"

Carry on like that for a bit. All along, strive to make your interaction with her come off like you have known her for a long time. Not like you just met her. After a while, say something like:

Her: Can I get you anything else?

You: "You know what? You're kinda cute. I think I'm going to call you..."

Her: You think so, huh? You don't have my number.

You: "Hey, you're right! Ok, give it to me and I'll write it down."

Her: (smiling) Not a good idea. I have a boyfriend.(or whatever objection; she surely won't give you her number right there in front of your friends)

You: (pretending to write) "Whoa, slow down. I didn't quite catch your number there. You better repeat it for me... let's see... 866..."

Her: (laughs and rolls her eyes)

The next night you go there again: Her: (laughing) Oh no! Not you again!

Mike: "Stephanie, my sweet! Hey listen, sorry I didn't return your call last night You know how it is. I'm just a busy guy."

Her: (playing along) Yeah, I'm really mad about that.

Later:

You: "You know what, Stephanie. You're a terrible girlfriend. In fact, I can't even remember the last time we had sex... That's it. We're through."

(pointing to another waitress) "I'm gonna find a new waitress to be my new girlfriend." (playing with your phone) "You're now downgraded from Booty Call #1 to Booty Call #10" Her: (laughing) No please, I'll do anything to make it up to you!

And later still:

Full Guide to Being Cocky and Funny

You: (motioning for her to come over and pointing at my knee) "Stephanie, come and sit down. I'll tell you a bedtime story."

Ok, now how do you transition from being a funny, ball-busting guy to a more serious, romantic, sexual state? Simple actually. At some point, just talk to her quietly alone. Remember to turn on the bedroom eyes:

You: (No longer c&f) "Stephanie, do you want me to call you?"

Her: You know I have a boyfriend.

You: "That's not what I asked. Do you want me to call you?"

Her: Tempting, but I can't...

...and run the usual game, routines, etc from there.

Stripper "Takedowns" and Tactics

If you're looking to pick up a stripper, do yourself a favor and go to the club on a night when the place isn't really busy. On weekends there are too many customers in the club, and the girls are basically stripping machines. They don't have time to sit and talk. The quieter the place is when you go, the more attention each girl will give you, and the more time you'll have to run game on her.

When you take a table and sit down, sit with your back to the stage and talk with your friends. This will make it look like you really don't care about any of the girls. If you go by yourself, get a table and sit sideways to the stage and only turn your head to look over for a few seconds every few minutes— concentrate on your drink. This will get the dancers thinking that you're interested more in a table dance, and they'll be quicker to approach you to ask.

When a girl does come around asking if you want to buy a dance, break the customer frame as quickly as possible. You don't want her to see you as just another 10$ bill. Go C&F: "You don't care about me! I'm just another 10$ bill to you! I can see dollar signs in your eyes when you look at me. Here, have a seat and talk with us and talk first." When she sits down beside you, DON'T turn your body to face her, just your head. She'll feel like she's not included in the group, and she'll probably work to gain rapport with you so she'll feel validated (AND try to get you to buy a dance). Go heavy with C&F on strippers, because you need to set yourself apart from all the ass-kissing guys saying how hot she is. Most importantly, don't compliment her on anything, and don't even acknowledge she's naked. Don't look her body over, don't even look down at her breasts even once. Just lock your eyes on her face, and pretend you're talking to some fully-clothed girl in a regular bar or club. If you comment on any props, accessories, or costumes she has, do it in a C&F way. Let's say she's wearing those shoes with the transparent plastic heels: "Ohhhh you're wearing glass slippers! That's so cute, you're like a little Cinderella". Eventually she'll ask you if you want to buy a dance. Tell her "Maybe later, we want to check out the other girls first". She'll leave flustered, but she'll be back in the hope of making some money off you later.

Never trust a stripper touching you as an indicator of interest. They rub you, touch you, caress you, etc. as a tactic to get you interested in a dance.

Most C&F and attraction techniques are just fine for using on dancers, since they are women after all. Here are some specific lines you can use in the strip club environment:

"What do you do? You're a dancer??? I thought you were just hanging out here naked!"

When she comes back and asks a second time if you want a dance: "There are all these beautiful girls in this room, why should I pick YOU?"

Flirty Statement of Intent (SOI): "Just because I don't want a dance doesn't mean I don't want you naked on top of me."

"What's the craziest thing you've ever done?" (blah blah) Turn your body away and act totally unimpressed at the answer. Then turn back, smile and say "Come on, are you JOKING?? The craziest thing you ever did was X??"

(if you've been gaming a dancer and she goes up to dance, DO NOT watch her. Turn your back to the stage and talk to your buddies. When she comes back to talk to you she'll ask why you weren't watching her) "Well I don't wanna watch you. Because we've been having such a nice conversation for (time) now and when I see you naked (notice the framing), I want it to be when we're all over each other like animals."

Cashier Strategies

"I could never have you as my girlfriend. There's not enough money in your tip jar to

Full Guide to Being Cocky and Funny

make my car payment."

"Thanks for the great service. This relationship is off to a great start."

(Using credit card with cashier) Act as if signing the receipt is you giving the cashier your autograph. For example, while signing your name, write something like: "To Debbie, for the jeans. Mike."

"So how much of this cash do you get to keep?" (as you hand her the money). She'll probably laugh and say: "None...I wish." To which you can respond with: "Oh, I thought you'd be pocketing 10 or 20%...I thought you were rich, but now I'm not interested...I want a rich girl." (Turn up your nose). She says "hey, I'm not rich but I AM nice/pretty/cool etc" say "Nice isn't good enough, I need rich AND nice."

Barmaid Strategies (from theplayersguide.com)

Seducing a barmaid is often a long-term project, so you have to ask yourself whether it's worth it. If you decide to go for it, here's a system:

Step 1: Smile, make sure to look straight into her eyes and ask her name before ordering a drink for the first time. Don't leave a big tip, instead leave a regular tip and buy her a drink. Go dance or work the club.

Step 2: Now that you know her name, always use it and smile whenever ordering drinks. Don't use words like "sweetie," "cutie," "baby," or "hey."

Step 3: In the beginning, never try to make conversation during hectic hours. You have to remember that she's very busy and needs to concentrate. The last thing she needs is a pest who makes her confuse the orders. Respect her zone and let her groove.

Besides, how interesting can you be if she has to interrupt you every two minutes? Your best bet is to show up early before the bar gets busy. This will give you more time to develop a conversation with her.

Step 4: Never volunteer your name; let her ask for it. It shows some sort of intrigue in what you have to say.

Step 5: No compliments -- everyone else has already let her know. To a barmaid, flattery means nothing. She hears it every night and has become immune to it -- especially from a stranger. Instead, give her a negative hit. Try saying something like, "Your lipstick is running," while smiling.

Step 6: Become her friend. That's right; don't show too much interest in her. Instead, concentrate on being a friend. I suggest you keep her entertained whenever she's not too busy.

Step 7: Have an interesting conversation; talk to her about something other than the bar scene. Ask her what she does in her leisure time. Ask if she has a day job or goes to school. Ask how her boyfriend handles so many men hitting on her (purpose -- to find out if she's available). The idea is to show authentic interest in her life, not her body.

Step 8: Dismiss any false buying signals. Remember, she might be flirting with you for a juicier tip. Look for other hints that might illustrate that she's not interested in your money.

Step 9: Asking for her phone number will lead her to believe that you are like all the others trying to get into her pants. Never ask for her digits; it's a dead giveaway that you're trying to pick her up.

Step 10: After developing a good friendship (usually takes a few weeks), ask what she's doing after work (assuming she has no boyfriend). Then ask if she'd like to go for coffee; if she's tired, ask if she'd like to hang out on a Sunday afternoon. If she says "no," at least you tried and won't have any regrets. If she says "yes," now is the right time to exchange phone numbers.

11. Wingman Strategies

A wingman, in fighter pilot lingo, is someone who covers your ass. In pick-up, it signifies a partner who helps you open sets, disarms obstacles, blocks potential cockblocks, and distracts the friends while you game the target. You can have more than one wingman in your group, but ideally you'll have one good PUA. More is not always better. For example, if you had 3 wingmen with you then opening a 4-set would be perfect at first glance. But let's say your target turns out to be a total dud! You can't switch your attention to anyone else in the set, so you're stuck—there's less flexibility. 2 PUAs with decent skills can usually keep a typical set occupied.

WINGMAN ETIQUETTE NEVER:

-Take your wingman's girl after he's gamed her

Full Guide to Being Cocky and Funny

-Move in on your wingman's target

-Blow your wingman's game by pointing out something negative about him or belittling him

ALWAYS:

-Talk strategy before a night out

-Decide beforehand who gets which target. If his sarge starts to go bad and his target begins to get cold to him, decide at what point you can move in.

-Let the man who opened a set target the hottest HB of the set, and lead the interaction.

-Talk up your wingman to a set (this guy is CRAZY sometimes, he's a lot of fun, etc). You REALLY have to do this, make him seem like the coolest guy in the world. Laugh at every joke he tells, within reason.

-Agree on signals for:

*   Telling your wingman to enter the set if you're having trouble handling it alone

*   ejecting from a set if either one senses it's a bad idea to continue (your wingman finds our they're both married for example)

*   showing your wingman which HB is your target when in set (if she's 3rd from the left for example, hold up 3 fingers while scratching your ear)

*   showing your wingman when a girl's buying temperature is going up and you plan to isolate her soon (the wingman can then start saying things to her friends like "Hey, let's go over here for a second", leaving you to game the target)

-Realize it's expected that you're going to have to "jump on the grenade" and occasionally get stuck with the "warpig" while your wingman games a hot target. Expect him to return the favour later! If he doesn't, find another wingman.

PIVOTS

A "pivot" is a female wingman, a "wingwoman" of sorts. The term pivot comes from your wingwoman opening a set or befriending a woman, and as she gets involved in convo you "pivot" around her and into set for her to introduce you.

If you can find a sociable female friend willing to be a pivot, your chances of success increase dramatically. Women will be less suspicious if a woman opens them, and then she can introduce you as a friend. This also gives the target a way around ASD (anti-slut defense) in that she can tell people she met you through a friend, instead of "he picked me up at a bar/on the street/whatever."

Pivots also provide SOCIAL PROOF. Social proof is the implication of a position of high social status. The better-looking the pivot, the higher your social proof will be. If your pivot is a solid 10, every woman will imagine you really must have something going for you to be in her company, and she'll want to know what that is. She "proves your social worthiness". Pivots don't necessarily have to be perfect 10s to be useful for social proof. Because a lot of women have a low self-image, a 10 may perceive herself as a 7 or an 8, so if your pivot is at least mildly attractive she should suit the purpose in most cases. Also, because of hot women's competitiveness, they may not be receptive to being opened by a 10-pivot.

12. Phase-Shifting to ATTRACT

At what point to you phase-shift to the ATTRACT phase? IMMEDIATELY after opening! The point of openers is to "open" a conversation with a woman and show originality, but that alone doesn't lead to anything unless you look like a movie star. You have to demonstrate value and convey your personality, and use social techniques to get her attracted to you. Otherwise you're just "shooting the shit."

Chapter 3

ATTRACT PHASE

Highlights:

1. Body language for attraction
2. Being a challenge
3. Engaging the competitive instinct
4. Being unpredictable and spontaneous
5. Being mysterious
6. Using Takeaways and Open Loops
7. Using Push/Pull
8. Using Role-Playing
9. Demonstrating higher social value
10. Showing indifference to her
11. Taking the lead
12. Using Cocky & Funny comments and themes
13. Using fluff talk to bridge between attraction points
14. Storytelling
15. Directing the conversation to sexual themes
16. Projecting Sexual State
17. Establishing dominance and dealing with tests
18. Dealing with poor behavior
19. Disarming obstacles
20. Dealing with "Let's Just Be Friends"
21. Advancing to Qualifying Her

The Attract phase is the MEAT of your interaction. It's fine to open a woman, it's fine to qualify her, it's find to develop rapport, but if you don't stir that emotion of ATTRACTION in her, all you're doing is making a new friend.

As David DeAngelo is quick to point out, ATTRACTION ISN'T A CHOICE. It's an unconscious response to certain personality characteristics and behavioral cues. If you simply hope that a woman will give you what you want by virtue of being around her, you'd better hope again. You have to do things to TRIGGER attraction. You have to demonstrate those behavioral cues.

Note that this section is a "how-to" guide for attraction. It tells you what to SAY and DO to demonstrate that you have attractive qualities. What's most important though is not what you say or do, but your ATTITUDE and the way you come across as you say or do it. Get your attitude/inner game spot-on, and it won't matter much WHAT you say or do.

Be the ALPHA male! In the animal kingdom, the Alpha male is the boss of the pack. He mates with most of the females in the pack, while the Beta males have a lower status and mate with few females, if any. Alpha indicates HIGH STATUS. You don't have to be a rich CEO or a rock star to have the MINDSET of the alpha male. Since you live in your own reality, realize you're the KING of YOUR reality! Hold the belief that you have extremely high social value and that you're the boss in your reality, and it'll come across in your interactions with women.

During the attract phase, try whenever possible to ISOLATE the target. If you're in a high-distraction area, invite her to go somewhere else where there are less distractions. If you've just met her on a busy sidewalk, invite her to a nearby coffee shop where people won't bump into her and break her attracted state. If you meet her at a noisy club, invite her somewhere else (terrace or quieter corner), and get her away from her friends. If you met her on a dance floor, move her up against the wall and away from the crowds.

Here's a playful intro for an isolation attempt: "Hey, come with me." (What? Where??) "I'm going to kidnap you to make your friends feel bad. No one will suspect it was me! Come on"

A note on attraction techniques

DON'T overdo any of the following techniques. There are so many guys who try to use humor and fun in an "exchange" frame with women—just like the guys who try to impress women with money. A few too many jokes and quips could be interpreted as an exchange frame gesture, like buying her drinks. You're trying to give value to her by being entertaining, and this can oversell the prospect (you). Tone it down and convey that it is YOU, a part of you, and not some kind of show. Be strong, never be submissive, don't become a song and dance show, be cool and relaxed, and

Full Guide to Being Cocky and Funny

CONSISTENT WITH THESE CHARACTERISTICS. Be playful (especially when you first meet a woman), but tone it down after a few minutes. At that point talk less, but when you do, make it count.

1. Body language and tonality for attraction

Good body language means having no nervousness or tension in your body. There are 3 types of body language: Macho, Good guy, and Nice guy. The Macho guy takes up LOTS of space, and looks like he's overcompensating for something. A Nice guy takes up as little space as possible and looks insecure and beta to others. The Macho guy façade will get you rejected just as much as the Nice guy façade. A "Good guy" is somewhere in between and projects a cool, relaxed image.

Using your body

*   Lean back
*   Take up space
*   Don't fidget, and be relaxed
*   Smile occasionally but not all the time, it looks insecure if you're constantly smiling
*   Slow down your movements...even BLINKING and looking around. Relax your breathing.
*   Always... eye contact, eye contact, eye contact! Use triangular gazing to amplify sexual state (looking softly from one eye to the other, to her lips, repeat)
*   Lean away from women when talking. Rarely lean in.

Use body language as a reward or punishment/take away. If she says something you approve of, move in closer or touch her briefly, or turn your body more to face her. If she says something that you disapprove of, lean back, cross your arms or take a step back, or turn your body more away from her.

Move into her and "slightly" intrude on her personal space. Move in and whisper in her ear if the place you're in is too loud. Have your lips "accidentally" brush her earlobe when you go to whisper in her ear.

If you're in a loud club, hold your drink close to your chest when talking to her. When you lean in to talk into her ear make it so that the outside of your forearm brushes against her breast gently and momentarily. You might find her starting to ask

Full Guide to Being Cocky and Funny

stupid questions just to have you lean in again!

If you're walking outside, have her lock elbows with you. This is powerful because it assumes that you're together.

Get noticed by your body language alone. Walk slowly, with your shoulders thrown back. Don't just walk, STRUT. Imagine the power you'd be walking with if you were the King of France, walking on a red carpet just for you. Hold your head high and make eye contact with people frequently.

Moving in set

Always remember that you need to keep MOVING while you're in set. Don't just walk up, plant yourself in front of the set, and game them stuck in place like a tree—you'll come off weird. One thing that ALL good PUAs do is simply that they are ALWAYS MOVING while in set. Backturns, taking a few steps back then forward (as if you're about to leave), sitting down, moving the set around, etc.

Voice tone and projection

The Macho/Nice/Good trinity also applies to voice quality. For instance, a low voice (Nice guy) shows meekness and nervousness, whereas an overly loud voice (Macho guy) shoes overcompensation and insecurity. Also, when it comes to voice and speech matters, you want to try and cut out "placeholder" words (words that you throw in while your brain tries to think of what to say next). Examples of this are "right," "um," and "you know."

Projecting your voice communicates strength and security, and people will take notice of you. It will allow you to take control of groups better, and is a very useful skill to have in a loud environment like a club or bar.

Also, work on speaking slower and deeper, and...using...PAUSES.

Body language and tonality troubleshooting

There are four major cues that show a lack of confidence:

1. Speaking too quickly. You want to speak powerfully and clearly, projecting your

voice. If you speak too quickly, it looks like you're just running your mouth and don't really know what to say.

2. Nervous energy. Having lots of nervous energy shows a serious lack of confidence, almost like you're not comfortable in your own body or nervous about talking to the girl. If you have this nervous energy, clasp your thumbs in you back pockets and lean back. This will make you look more laid back and relaxed even if you are screaming with terror on the inside.

3. Laughing at your own jokes. The last cue that gives away a lack of confidence is laughing at your own jokes. Laughing at your own jokes undermines the humor and makes it look like you're trying too hard to be funny. Allow others to determine what's funny and judge them on it. If you laugh at stuff that isn't funny, you look like a tool.

4. Nervous ticks and fidgeting. You may APPEAR calm and confident when talking to a woman, but if your foot is shaking, you're gritting your teeth, or you're tapping the table it'll give away the fact that you're nervous. Work to eliminate these habits from your normal behaviors.

Tonality shifts are huge in all interactions with chicks at any stage. You don't want to be that boring guy. Change things up!

2. Being a challenge

When a girl asks you what you did yesterday, never say, "Oh, I just sat around and was bored." Better to say, "I was up early to run errands and take care of business, then worked out, met a friend for supper, and went to work." Lie if you have to. And don't worry, you'll get used to it! "Fake it til you make it"

If a girl calls and asks what you are doing, reply with, "I just walked in the door" or "I'm just on my way out to take care of some things."

Don't hang on the phone for hours talking to girls indicating you don't have anything else to do. Get the business of the call over, be pleasant, then excuse yourself. Always try to get off the phone first.

By not calling a girl every night or contacting her every day, you show that you are busy and have other things that are important in your life besides her. This lets her know that she is going to have to compete for your time. Don't always return calls promptly.

If you run into her in public, be pleasant and friendly. Show her that you have an interest in her, but then excuse yourself because of having things to do. In this way, you show her that she is going to have to work for your time. You are not "easy."

By letting people know that you are a person doing things and active, you suggest a lot to a girl. Certainly, you must be someone who knows where you are going, hence, leadership. You play on her sense of wanting w hat she can't have because she will have to compete for your time with all of your other activities. You will appear to be different from all the other guys who are hanging on her begging for her time. She will suspect that there are other girls in your life or you wouldn't be so busy. And finally, she is going to have to use her charms to seduce you away from all these other activities - and girls just love a challenge.

Make her miss you. But in order for scarcity to be effective you have to be sure of one thing. The time she does spend with you must be absolutely amazing, and without a doubt the best time she could have with anyone. You need to be able to create an awesome, MEMORABLE experience with anyone, anywhere, especially when it really counts.

Also, she can NEVER be the first priority in your life. Always put her second to something, whether it be your family, career, friends, whatever, but leave a small piece of hope in her mind that she could become #1.

When dealing with women, DON'T OVERSELL! Don't try too hard to attract and impress. When it shows you're trying too hard, bragging, etc, you're not a challenge, you're the one trying to prove your worth! Stay relaxed, and make the few actions and words you use COUNT. Try not to say more than two sentences in a conversation before you allow her to respond, and no more than five when telling a story.

3. Engaging the competitive instinct

Part of being a challenge is bringing out women's natural competitive instinct. Women want what other women have! Married men will tell you that they get more attention from women than when they were single. They're a CHALLENGE!

If you have a hickey, claw-marks on your back, get caught with lipstick on your collar, etc., say to the woman who noticed "Well, the ladies are marking their territory". Don't be all embarrassed and apologetic for it. You don't have to be exclusive with a woman to whom you have no commitment.

Create competition in the eyes of girlfriends by telling them when meeting their friends "I think your friend has a crush on me".

In your small talk, discretely drop hints that you have women in your life, possibly as more than friends. "My friend is supposed to come over tonight. *SHE* wants to watch a movie or something. But if she can't make it, I'll probably be going downtown."

If the conversation gets on dating and relationships (Which it will, because you will LEAD it there), throw in:

"When I'm talking to girls and they ask me if I have a girlfriend, they seem really shocked when I say that I'm single." She'll pick up on the subcommunication: She KNOWS that when a girl asks a guy if he has a GF, that's an Indicator of Interest. She understands that these girls are attracted to you. This creates implied SOCIAL PROOF.

When asked if you see other women, never answer directly. Deflect with humor and say something like "No, other MEN" or "THOUSANDS. In fact while you were just in the bathroom I banged one of them." If she just won't leave you alone about it: "Well, yes I do go out with a lot of girls because I'm picky". Wait for her to talk. She'll most likely say: "How can you be picky if you go out with a lot of girls? It doesn't make sense." This is where you'll win her over by saying: "When I find the girl who can keep me interested then I'll stay with her. I need to go out with different girls to give myself a chance of finding her. Otherwise I'd have to just stay at home and I'll never meet my dream girl will I?" By ending this with "will I?" you put her in a position where it is her turn to answer and any reasonable, thinking woman will agree with what you're saying.

4. Being unpredictable and spontaneous

Inconsistency is the key to driving her desire up. Consistency only sends messages to her subconscious that you are a man she could RELY on, but that doesn't make her LUST after you. You can use an analogy of rides at an amusement park: Consistency and predictability is the Ferris wheel. Ho hum. Boring. You go up, and around, and back down ... and up.... Nothing fast. Nothing unknown. Just a tall view and look around the area. Nice, but NO thrills. Inconsistency - Surprise, danger, thrills - are found on the ROLLER COASTER. Get her in the front car and start her heart racing with the unknown. You have to get her on the right ride if you want to get where you want to go. Keep her off balance, so she doesn't know what's coming.

5. Being mysterious

Being mysterious doesn't mean faking that you work for the CIA and keep everything a secret. It simply means not being an open book. If you knew ahead of time how a movie ended, you probably wouldn't be as interested in it. It's the same thing with mystery; by maintaining an air of mystery about something, whether it be about yourself, an event, or your past, you invoke a woman's curiosity and keep her interested.

Too much disclosure by YOU too early kills (MURDERS!) your chances for sleeping with a woman. Too much disclosure means you lack SELF-CONTROL, and that's one of the critical components of your self-confidence. It's better to err to the side of giving her too little information. It creates more mystery, which works in your favor (as long as you work to increase her attraction along with it). Telling her something negative about you can NEVER increase the positive feelings she has for you. It doesn't work like that. Don't be a disclosure machine! Leave some questions unanswered. You can actually use bits of disclosure as a reward method when she does something you approve of.

She asks you what you did last Saturday: "That's classified".

She asks you something about your past: "I'll tell you when I know you better" (a challenge for her, because it gives her something to strive for—earn your trust/get the details)

She asks how many women you've slept with: "Wouldn't YOU like to know that? Heheh"

She asks what you two are doing Friday night: "It's a surprise".

Tell her "I have something for you". When she asks, don't tell her no matter how hard she pushes. It can be something as simple as a kiss, but she won't know that until you see her.

6. Using takeaways and open loops

Takeaways involve getting her really into something you're saying or doing, and then literally taking it away. Say she's laughing and enjoying herself with you and you unexpectedly say "I have to go see my friends, I'll be back in a few minutes". That's a takeaway. You show open and receptive body language to her while you talk, then lean back and cross your arms unexpectedly, or turn your back on her to focus on a distraction. That's a takeaway. This is the idea behind ending interactions first, and on a positive note. As the saying goes, ALWAYS LEAVE THEM WANTING MORE.

Takeaways can be used as a system of reward and punishment as well. Reward positive behavior by giving her value and attention, punish negative behavior by taking it away.

Open loops are similar to takeaways, but involve leaving something unresolved. An example of an open loop would be telling a woman, "I've been meaning to tell you something all night. I think you're…Hold on, I think I just saw someone I know, I'll be right back." OR as she's talking just interrupt with "You know, I just realized something about you." When she says "What?" say "….I'll tell you later." And just smile. Resist her attempts to pry it out of you and change the subject. Another example of an open loop would be calling a woman's answering machine and leaving the following partial message: "Hi HB,
I have the funniest story to tell you about last night! It all started when this bum came up to me on the street. And then he held up this cat that only had 3 legs… Anyway, call me". Another open loop example: When you see she's getting involved and really interested in some idea or story you're telling, change the subject with no warning.

The whole purpose behind an open loop is to get the HB interested in the outcome, then avoid disclosing it. Just like you stay and watch a shitty show just to see how it ends, people will listen to your shitty story just to see how it ends. If the conclusion is withheld they'll feel a bit cheated, and may want to hear it to the point of a minor obsession. This is why soap operas have hooked women for decades; the shows never truly conclude, and always end with open loops. Open loops cause frustration, and the person will then crave emotional relief. By withholding that relief you build up tension.

Here are some more examples of open loops:

"SOMETHING ABOUT YOU" OPEN LOOPS While telling a woman a story, say something like: "I bet you like attention", or "I bet you were a daddy's girl" Then resume your story. Now if you've peaked her interest, she'll interrupt you. If you haven't, just keep making comments like this until she takes the bait. When she takes the bait, she'll be thinking to herself, "What does he mean by that?" (This is great because it gets them interested on an EMOTIONAL level). She'll interrupt you with, "What do you mean by that?"

Retort with something like "Didn't your mom teach you any manners? It's rude to interrupt someone while they're talking. But I know this because you remind me of my...well I will tell you later" and then resume telling the rest of your story.

"SHE WANTS TO TELL YOU SOMETHING INTERESTING" OPEN LOOPS When she tells you she has something interesting/exciting/etc to tell you, say "I'm busy right now but that sounds interesting, why don't you tell me when we get together?"

NUMERICAL OPEN LOOPS "There are 3 things I look for in a woman". Then only tell her two!

SILENCE OPEN LOOPS When she's trying to explain or justify something, be silent and unexpressive. She'll wonder if you agree with her or not and try harder to explain herself.

GETTING HER TO SAY "WHAT" OPEN LOOPS Say "you're such a girl" and when she says "What? What is it?" just smile and change the subject or look away.

7. Using Push/Pull

In the game of attraction, if you try to pull someone closer to you, they'll resist. And if you try to push them away from you, they'll want you because you're a challenge. Doing both (within limits) can be emotionally confusing to a woman, and this builds tension.

Full Guide to Being Cocky and Funny

Push/pull can be described simply through the following phrase: "I like you...I don't like you...Wait, I think I like you....Nahh, I don't like you....Actually, now that I think about it, I like you! Well...I'm not sure..."

By constantly giving approval (pulling) and then taking it back (pushing), you're leaving ambiguity in your communication and driving the woman crazy. Here's some examples of push/pull in action:

"You know, you're kinda cute. I think you'd make a nice girlfriend. WAIT, can you cook? I need a woman who can cook! Oh, you can? Great! I'm impressed. BUT what kind of food do you cook? Oh, Thai? I'm not sure I like Thai. What else can you cook? Italian? Now we're talking! I like you already! BUT can you cook GOOD Italian food is the question."

"You're my new girlfriend." (pause) "No, I changed my mind, we're broken up." (why) "You're too nice for me...look at you, you're already IN LOVE with me...you don't even know me!" (OMG hahahaha, No I'm not!) "Just look at your body language, man...laughing at all my dumb jokes, falling in love..."

Another example, that's more serious: "Oh, you have a Masters degree in   ? Great, I LOVE smart women! They're fun to be around. But are you TOO intellectual? I'm not crazy about women who are too intellectual, they're not as fun. But I find the field of very interesting, so it would be fun to get to know you I'm sure."

A process like this gets her thinking "Oh, a compliment...I've got him! Ummm..maybe not. Oh wait, he DOES like me. Aww no that's not good enough for him. So does this guy like me or not?"

You can also use your body language for push-pull purposes. Communicate interest one minute by leaning forward, showing enthusiasm, etc, then show indifference the next minute by leaning back, crossing your arms, looking bored, turning your body away from her, etc.

Push/pull is a fine art that needs to be used with caution. Watch your target's reaction and make sure you're not going too far. She should be a little frustrated by your ambiguous behavior (this frustration builds sexual tension), but if she's showing anger you're probably pushing it too far. Here are some more examples of push/pull: GUILTY CONSCIENCE: Provoke her into doing something, then make her feel guilty about it. She goes to kiss you: "I can't kiss you, you're like my little sister! That would be like incest." Then pull her to you and kiss her.

BREAKING RAPPORT: Show that you CAN connect with her on some topic, and when she gets into it, change the topic.

GOOD COP/BAD COP: Being mean or condescending but then following it up immediately with a nice estimation. Gets her seeking validation. "You're so X. You know, I usually don't get involved with women who are X, but you have a great way of looking at the world so it's cool, we can hang out."

INTENTIONAL UNDERMINING: "You have SUCH a gorgeous smile." (Thank you). "Actually I know four other people who have really nice smiles, so I'm going to call you number 5."

UNDERMINING RAPPORT: Once rapport is established, say something like "You and I are too alike, we'd never be able to hang out together".

If she wants to wear your jacket/hat/etc: "You have to be very special to wear this hat" Give it to her for a 30-second trial period, then pull it away and make her re-earn it. "Time's up!"

8. Using Role-Playing

Role-playing involves finding a humorous situation and then projecting the two of you into that "role". It's very powerful because #1 it's FUN, and #2 it projects the 2 of you doing things together in the future (even though the situations are clearly fictional). Here are some examples of role-plays you could use:

Vegas wedding role-play

-You're pretty cool. We should get married. Right now. Let's go to Las Vegas and get married! It was good enough for Britney Spears, it's good enough for us!
-There's a plane leaving for Vegas in 2 hours. I checked!

Full Guide to Being Cocky and Funny

-We'll get Little Richard himself to marry us. Or do you prefer Elvis?
-Since we're gonna annul the marriage after, we have to follow the rules:
So we can't have any sexual contact! (Awwwww) Ok, well maybe some heavy petting and a hickie then.
-We could have our honeymoon in Fiji! And we can stay in those grass huts that stand over the water.

-Actually FORGET the grass huts...our wedding night activities would tear the hut to shreds! And we'd get grass stains all over our NAKED bodies from all the friction! (If she brings up the no sex annulment rule, say "Well the judge won't know we did anything when we go for the annulment")
-Remember, we're only gonna be married for about 2 weeks, so don't make too many plans!

If going for a walk later, and there's a church nearby...

-(So what are we doing now?) Well I thought we were gonna get married??
-We don't need Vegas, its' the same thing anyway...instead of being married by a man in an elvis costume we'll be married by a man in a DRESS...instead of carrying you across the threshold in a cheap motel room in Vegas, it'll be a cheap motel downtown

-Come with me, there's a church down the street

(Walk to the nearest Church...If your meeting takes place at night there'll be a 90% chance that the doors will be locked). This is BULLSHIT man! Churches are getting terrible hours, they're worse than banks these days!!!

(If you happen to find that the church is open, and you have the balls to pull this off, go in with her and talk to the minister!)

Good evening Pastor/Reverend/Father, we're looking to book a wedding. (when?) Well, as soon as possible (In three weeks in the afternoon blah blah) Can't it be any sooner? (blah blah) This is a nice church, it must be expensive for a wedding ceremony here? (gives price) Oww...Do you offer financing? What's your APR? (blah blah) Ok, we'll go check with another church and come back...we'll do some price-shopping. Thanks for your time Pastor/Reverend/Father!

Full Guide to Being Cocky and Funny

(To girl after leaving) See? You have to price shop! These (Baptist, Anglican, whichever denomination) people will rip you off! Ok forget the church, all we need is a minister! We need to find a priest walking around downtown on a Friday night... Or a JUDGE!! A judge could marry us! We need to find a judge.

Hey I have an idea!! Let's have raw, dirty, public sex right here in the street! We'll be in front of a judge in no time!! (of course the woman will say no) Ok fine let's smash some windows, boost a car....then smash it into the back of a police car!

Ok ok forget the wedding for tonight, we'll get married tomorrow. I'm gonna have my bachelor party tonight, and you're invited! Now let's go get loaded and see some strippers!!! (she says she wants to have a bachelorette party) Well, you'll need to find a male stripper for a bachelorette party, might be kinda tough at this late hour... I volunteer!

Barbie and Ken role-play

"Look at us! We're sooo cool. We're like Barbie and Ken!" (call her Barbie the rest of the night, and get her to call you Ken). "I'll be your Ken doll! Actually I have an advantage over Ken dolls." (What?) "Ken Dolls don't come FULLY EQUIPPED!"

"We can have our own Barbie House...In the summer we can hold a Barbie Barbecue in the backyard, with that fake plastic meat on it. And our own Barbie camper...And you could have that pink Barbie Corvette so you can drive me around in style! And we can ride with the top down with these fake plastic smiles stuck to our faces! (Make really fake smile and hold it till she cracks up). Come on, let's see YOUR fake plastic smile! (Push her until
she does it, and you'll both crack up together).

If she complains about not being beautiful enough, or she's not blonde, tell her "It's okay! You don't have to be blonde and perfect to be Barbie! You can be the new 'politically correct' Barbie! The Barbie who gets zits sometimes...who has trouble walking in high heels...and suffers from PMS! Look at ME for example. I'm playing Ken, do I look perfect to you?" (bust on her playfully if she answers anything other than yes)

Sacrilege role-play

Full Guide to Being Cocky and Funny

Hey I got a great idea to pass the time! (what) I dress up like a priest...You dress up as a nun...then we go to mass on Sunday, and just to freak everyone out we'd just start MAKING OUT. What do you think, "Sister"?

Simple name role-play

"If you were a man, what name would you want to have?" Then call her by that name from then on. She'll ask you back, so have an answer ready and be prepared to have her call you it back when you use HER 'opposite sex name'.

PVC Devil role-play (for use with 2-sets)

"Oh, you're getting fiesty huh? You know what I'd do with you? I'd dress you up.... in a red.. PVC... DEVIL outfit.. You'd have little horns like this... and a tail.. bitch boots, and..... a pitch fork. Now your friend here.. I'd dress her up in a similar angel outfit.. with wings.. and a fur halo.. and I'd roll with you guys on each arm down the street.. Every girl would be jealous of you.. And whenever I'd have to make a decision.. I'd let each of you fight over
which decision is the most fun.. and whatever one would be the most fun.. we'd do that." (the periods are to show the pacing, because they roll over laughing in between every pause)

Use this role-play early on in set, or later on in set before you're about to move them. It implants the idea of rolling on each arm, and then you throw out your arms and they jump on them like magnets.

Bodyguard role-play

If she acts or talks tough, or talks about pushing/punching/kicking some loser/ex-boyfriend who was making a play for her, say "Wow, you're tough! I'm hiring you as my new BODYGUARD." If she has pointy shoes on, add "With THOSE shoes you'd be leaving guys on the floor all over the place....holding their balls and groaning in pain." Tell her "I can't pay you much, but the benefits are GREAT." (What are the benefits?) "Well, you get to spend a lot
of time hanging out with ME." If you two are going places, tell her to walk ahead of you to make sure it's safe. You can take this wherever you want to go with it, since the premise of "guarding your body" can lead to all sorts of things. And if you're dealing with a groupset: "You guys are TOUGH. I'm making you my bodyguards! Just

like protecting the President...You're my VICTORIA'S-SECRET SERVICE. You guys can run alongside my presidential limo in high heels and skimpy lingerie."

Political role-play

If she happens to show some interest in politics and it's around election time: "You know, I think both the political candidates we have are CRAP. We should run for office, you and I. I'll be the President and you'll be my running-MATE. But actual mating is optional, of course..." If she resists: "Come on, you know this country could use a FEMALE vice-president! And if you ever wanted to become FULL president, all you'd have to do is arrange my assassination." Keep pushing her until she agrees, then say "Ok, I accept you as my running-mate. But I have to warn you, there's a lot of hard campaigning ahead... A LOT of late nights." If she resists, finally say "Ok, if you're not going to be my vice-president, then at least I'll make you one of my bodyguards." Then go into the bodyguard role-play and bring up "Victoria's-Secret Service". By the way, this isn't limited to Presidential campaigns; you could insert whatever political position suits the discussion (mayor, governor, etc). And you don't have to do this around campaign time either; just get on the topic of what a shitty job the (mayor, president, etc) is doing, and say "You know, in the next election, WE should run for office."

Space escape role-play

If a woman is bitching and complaining about something, be it work, studies, money problems, the state of the world, etc., cut her off with the following role play (and you should ALWAYS try to cut off complaining and bitching as quickly as possible, so she doesn't link a negative state to you): "You know, I'm fed up with things here too. Let's escape to outer space. You and I, we'll go to Cape Canaveral and steal the Space Shuttle...Then we'll fly it to the moon and set up our own little colony...We'll populate it with 10,000 babies...and we can keep in touch with our friends and family through e-mail". If she freaks at the thought of 10,000 babies, just say "Well there isn't much else to do on the moon, it's not a very exciting place." This is a pretty limited role-play, but it's ridiculous enough to break her state and get her off the negative topic. And after this, anytime she tries to bring it up again, you can cut her off with "I told you! We need to escape to the moon! Complaining about it is NOT the solution."

Swinggcat's Good Doggie role-play

Full Guide to Being Cocky and Funny

A ROLE-PLAYING scenario that's lots of fun to do with a woman is to ask her: "If you were a dog, what kind of dog would you be and why?"

After she answers, say "I like that kind of dog. I might have to buy you from the pet store."

Then say with a suspicious look on your face, while almost turning your back on her, "You don't pee on the floor, d o you?"

If she says "no" then grab her hands while pulling them in close and say, "Good, then I'm taking you home with me".

Then look in her eyes, hold her hands but start to push her just a wee bit away from you, and say "Are you an adventurous doggie? Because if not I'm going to take you to the pound".

If she says that she is, pull her even closer to you and say, "Good doggie" (you might even want to pat her on the head at this point).

Then hug her and tell her that she's such a cute doggie. Then say to her, "You know why?" She'll say, "why". Say "Because you remind me of Sammy." She'll ask, "Who's Sammy?" Respond by telling her that Sammy was the only dog that you ever loved, but he had to be put down, and since she's almost as cute as Sammy you're going to name her "Number Two".

Then grab her really close as if you're going to kiss her, look in her eyes, and say: "Ew... you're trying to kiss me and you're a dog!!!"

The "Would You" Game

Closely related to role-playing is the "Would You" game. Ask her how much money it would take for her to (be a stripper, change the oil in my car, have sex with an 80 year-old man, etc). Whatever she says, try to talk her down in price!

The real beauty of role-plays is that you can easily use "call-back humor" with them. Next time you call her you can say "Hi! It's your future temporary husband" or "Hey Barbie! It's Ken". This can instantly get her in the fun state created by your prior role-play and start the conversation off playfully.

9. Demonstrating higher social value than her

"The only rule in pick-up is to always be visibly cooler than the chick you're trying to game." –Tyler Durden, Cliff's List

Don't ever let her show you up. ALWAYS maintain the upper hand. If she makes you look like a fool because you have no comeback or look weak, the target becomes more cool than you and you're in a position of weakness.

When you're in her presence, you should never treat her like you desperately want and need her approval. Whatever you do, don't try to "impress" her, act apologetic for anything about yourself, or otherwise give away your personal POWER. EVER.

Demonstrate leadership and show AUTHORITY in everything you do. Women are universally not attracted to passive, ass-kissing, weak men. The slightly overconfident, cocky man conveys higher social value.

Never give a woman what she asks for, except on your terms. That includes answers to her questions.

Patronizing comments can also be used to knock a woman off her pedestal and show her that you aren't intimidated/have higher value:

"You know what? You impress me. You're A-crowd." "Wow, you're sooo cool. Can I be your friend?"
"You're so cool. I'm gonna adopt you." "You're so cute, you're like a little puppy"
"You're sooo cute, you're like Sailor Moon without all the martial arts"

10. Showing indifference to her

You must show that you don't NEED her. As for wanting her, keep her guessing on whether you want her or not. Act like you don't care if she rejects you or not, act like you could walk away at any moment and not be bothered.

More importantly, don't push a woman for anything. You must give an unusually attractive woman SPACE. You can't call her every day, tell her that you're in love with her two days after you've met her, chase her around, always ask what she's doing, etc. You must give this special woman THE GIFT OF MISSING YOU.

If you have a life, stay with it. If you don't have a life, get one. Don't sit around wondering what she's doing, calling her, telling her how you "feel", etc. If she wanted another "girlfriend", she'd get one. So don't act like one. Desirable women want men who are INDEPENDENT, and who give them SPACE. In fact, if anything, you need to give a hot woman TOO MUCH space. You want HER to be the one who is calling YOU to figure out what you're up to.

11. Taking the lead

Always take the lead. Women are attracted to dominant men who are leaders. They're universally NOT attracted to weak, ass-kissing, supplicating men.

Never ask for anything (it gives the woman the power). Use soft commands instead. (NOT "Can I have your number?" but instead "Hey, what's your number"; NOT "Will you dance with me?" but instead "Come on, let's dance" as you take her by the hand and lead her).

Another way to get something is to structure opportunities and offer challenges-It gives YOU the power. If she doesn't accept the opportunity or challenge, she misses out! Never ask her for anything, instead suggestively entice and let her give to you.

Never give her anything, instead reward her. If she will not give you anything, give her a reason to, or challenge her to, or dare her to. Be decisive and show that you're in control. Show that you have AUTHORITY in all situations. Make the decisions as often as possible (including FOR HER when it's feasible—like ordering her a drink at the bar).

12. Using cocky & funny comments and themes

Using humor is golden. "If you get 'em laughing, the rest is easy".

The best approach is using humor combined with a bit of cockiness, to flirt with them while teasing them. This sends all the right signals. In effect, it tells a woman, "I'm not intimidated by you and your beauty doesn't scare me. In fact, I'm so comfortable around you that I can even make fun of you in a friendly way."

Full Guide to Being Cocky and Funny

Although David DeAngelo recommends keeping a serious face while doing C&F, I've found that a slight hint of sarcasm and a smirk along with the comment has more of an impact. It also makes you look like you're playful, and it doesn't paint you as an a**hole.

Some examples of C&F:

Reach your hand out to help her out of your car or something. Hold her hand for a second longer than pull it away, saying "Hey, no hand-holding this early"

Tells you about a club or hangout she goes to: "It can't be that cool" (why not?) "Because I've never heard of it".

"Look, just because you're being sweet to me doesn't mean I'm going to sleep with you. You thought I was THAT easy? Come on!"

(with women at work or women working somewhere) "How can you possibly get any work done when you're flirting with me all the time? I know I'm a stud and all but if you lose your job, don't think I'm going to support you!"

(after seeing a woman) "I know we had fun, but please don't become a stalker and call me 50 times a day"

(how are you?) "Well, I've been told I'm pretty damn good!"

(If she makes fun of herself) Her: "I'm such a retard" or "My hair looks awful" or "My lipstick doesn't look good does it?" You: "Well, I didn't want to say anything!"
OR
Her: "My hair looks bad doesn't it?"
You: "You can say that again!" (with a playful tone)

"I have to go and get ready." (where are you going?) "You're taking me for a drink".

Her: "Does my hair look better up or down?" You: "It looks bad both ways"
Her: "HEY!" *punch* etc..

"You can keep being cold, but I know that deep down, you love me."

Full Guide to Being Cocky and Funny

"Come on, have you sat down with a SEXIER man than ME today? Be honest." "You don't get a chance like this everyday...to hang out with a hot guy like ME."

(What kind of woman do you respect?) "Ones that don't ask a lot of questions."

(asks you what your plans are for X day) "NO, you CAN'T take me to Vegas and marry me!" Can lead to Vegas Wedding role-play.

"Wow, that's an ugly shirt/skirt etc. How long til the bet wears off?" (HEY!) "That's what happens when you get high before you go shopping"

(How's your love life?) "Have you ever heard of James Bond? You get the idea." OR (So, are you seeing anyone special?) "What do you mean by "special?" No, I wouldn't call any of them "special"... unless you're talking about not being the sharpest tool in the shed... in that case, yes, I'm seeing a couple of 'special' women."

(Goes to hug you) "Look at you, you're all over me!"
"Does it upset you to be walking with such a sexy man because nobody is looking at you, and everyone's looking at me?"

"I know you want me for my sexy body, but I'm tired of feeling like just an object to women. I'm tired of women always staring at me and wanting my body."

"I'm impressed. Normally, women like you are intimidated by my charm and good looks"

(Customer service girl) "Wow, thanks for your help... I think this relationship is off to a good start."
(3rd party: So how do you two know each other?) "We're actually brother and sister." Then start fondling her and say "Our relationship is a bit incestuous."

(invitation to her place) "What?? I don't even know you and you want me at your place already? Sorry I'm not that easy. Whatever happened to the good old days when ladies invited guys for coffee first?"

"Look I know how you women are: First a little compliment, then phone number, then back to your place to check out your stereo...I'm not like that!"

Full Guide to Being Cocky and Funny

"What makes you think I WANT to sleep with you?" (What??) "I think you need to change the battery on your Miracle Ear."

A good Cocky & Funny theme to follow is "You're screwing up your chances with me", "This relationship just isn't going to work", "What did I tell you about this kind of behavior?". In other words, you're communicating the very OPPOSITE of "You're a potential wife or girlfriend".

A little harsh, but good if she's got a mega bitch-shield, "I'm hot and I know it" attitude. "You don't know what sexy is... look at you, you're trying too hard, you look like a little girl playing dress up. REAL sexiness doesn't come from wearing make up or tight clothes...you're probably even uncomfortable in those clothes...It comes from inside, being in touch with that natural woman inside of you..."

"Hey, what's with the big purse? You're not one of those women with a live dog named "Precious" in there, are you?"

(You're crazy) "I'm a little unconventional...and I'm definitely NOT predictable! But I'm not crazy. Well, I can get a LITTLE crazy...in bed!"

"Look how happy you are to (hear from/see/be with) me! You LOVE me!"

(You're so   ) "The question is, do you find   sexy, or IRRESISTABLY sexy??"

"Don't think I'm EASY! You have to work for me!"

(uses your bathroom, gone for a long time) When she comes back say, "You're not some Al-Qaeda member trying to plant a bomb in my house, are you?"

If she has really rigid posture, pull your shoulders back, sit up extra straight, and say "I really think you should work on your posture." (I like you more and more everyday) "DAMN you're slow... everyone else falls for me right away, what's taking you so long?"

Every time she passes you, say loudly "Will you stop grabbing my ass!"

"I hate you.. Actually wait, that may have come across wrong. I really really hate you. You know why? You remind me of Justine from Grade 2. She always beat me at hot hands. Here, let's see.." and then play hot hands. If you beat her: "Ok I don't hate you, because I can beat you at hot hands". If she beats you (which shouldn't happen, you're a man dammit!) say "See? I knew I was right to hate you! You beat me at hot hands."

"Hey, no groping" (after she touches you)

(Says something intelligent) "Hey, you're pretty smart...For a GIRL!"

"I could marry a woman like you." (really?) "I'd divorce you a week later and take half your money."

If she still lives at home, tease her about being grounded or having a curfew

C&F Responses to compliments

"Wow, you're really into me aren't you?

"Look, I'm not like other guys. This compliment thing isn't going to get you anywhere."

"Already starting with the compliments, huh? Look, let's just get this over with... go buy me the drink already."
"I'm not giving you my phone number, so just stop with the compliments." "Come on, can't you at least think of something original to compliment me on?"

"I'm cute? You're cute too. What do you wanna do about it?"

(Nice shirt/pants/etc) "Thanks! Would you like to take it off me?"

(You're so   ) "Just giving the public what it wants."

(You're so   ) "I'm glad you noticed. I realize that this is making you very attracted to me, but please...control yourself."
(You have nice muscles) "You know, I'm really tired of you women treating me like some kind of piece of meat. I have feelings too, I'm not just a sex object."

Full Guide to Being Cocky and Funny

(If she implies you're a gentleman) "Do you consider me GENTLE? I'll have to spank you more often then!"

"Caveman" C&F

"Cavemanning" is a form of playful physical teasing. It's basically cocky kinesthetics/kino. It includes:

-Play fighting
-Giving her a light punch to her arm. If she punches back, "Owwwwww. That's my WEAK arm!!" This will really crack her up if you're very built.
-Hockey body checking her
-Picking up something small and swatting her with it! A napkin, straw, etc
-Flicking water at her
-Tickle attack!
-Slapping her butt if she's being a brat
-Throwing her over your shoulder and walking away with her ("I'm taking you home, you don't know how to act in public!")

If she's getting flustered and asks "Why I am talking to you??" "Because you LOVE me!" (blah blah denial) "Of course! I see it in your eyes!" (check her eyes, pull her eyelids down like a doctor) "Yup, it's pretty obvious".

"Hey did you know that they say you need 11 hugs a day to stay healthy?" Joke about her hug shortage, lack of physical contact, etc. Do a "massage- hug", then: "Ohhh...I don't know if you DESERVE a massage yet"

Overdoing it (Tyler Durden, Cliff's List)

Too much cockiness will make you look insecure and arrogant, and too much humor makes you look goofy. You also risk crossing the line into making her feel ridiculed. If C&F goes too far, immediately follow with "You know, I'm so sorry. I'm a total dick sometimes. People think I'm a dick sometimes, because I'm always messing around. I like you. You're like my bratty little sister. Sorry for being a dick." Say this *sincerely*, but from a position of authority. Like your vocal tonality isn't seeking approval in any way. Then follow it up with a field tested funny story to diffuse the tension.

Full Guide to Being Cocky and Funny

TURNAROUND STRUCTURE

1- Don't acknowledge that she's even pissed. Don't show any facial expressions of reaction to her getting upset. Laugh it off, but in a way where you're not laughing to cover up discomfort. Like you think she's almost joking or teasing. This is important, because if she thinks you realized she was serious, it's natural psychology to be consistent to it and not let it go.

2- Interpret it like she just qualified herself to you, in the way that she showed that she can stick up for herself. Do this in a funny way, using funny mini-cold- reads or future adventures projections.

3- Give a brief sincere apology from a position of authority.

4- Follow up immediately with something funny or intriguing to distract her. "Change her mood not her mind." "I grew up with a sister, and teasing was a form of affection" "We're like Sam and Diane from Cheers"

Another concept is that when you heat up the situation, people will crave rapport. The feel the emotional/psychological heat of the interaction, and they want relief of discomfort. Your "apology" and change of subject provides that relief.

Grandmaster Style—Sexually Overt C&F (From alt.seduction.fast)

GM style explained

Contributed to ASF (alt.seduion.fast) by Nathan Szilard, this is the description of the technique used by a pickup artist acquaintance of his nick- named Grand Master Flash's. Hence the name GM technique. The key here is smutty sex jokes and continuous humorous sex-talk with keen attention to how the girl reacts, so as to forestall any negative reactions (and you can be sure, there will be plenty in the beginning!) by saying "just kidding", giving an "apologetic" hug to the girl etc. The reasoning here is this, that if the girl has
no chance to express her negative comments about sex-jokes and -comments, this translates in her subconscious to agreeing and accepting what is being said. The

defenses will eventually go down, she has to imagine all the sex-jokes in her mind in order to understand them, and although she might be disgusted or repelled about them in the first place, she won't be able to express her negativism, her mind is bombarded with more sexual references, she just keeps imagining and before she knows it, nature kicks in and... she's getting horny! Simple. But potentially dangerous as hell - you really need to be in your element with all the sex jokes and keep "just kidding" in time not to get slapped in the beginning etc. Otherwise you could fail miserably.

Nathan Szilard on GM Flash and his technique, ASF: "That's his aggressive style. Basically he told them he wanted to fuck from the beginning. He had the attitude that he could satisfy them sexually. He had the confidence that says he does this all the time. He was in their face. He was making them excited. He was stimulating them like they are not USED TO being stimulated. If they were going to resist, they would have resisted when he first told them what he wanted from them. There is the INCORRECT assumption that chicks don't like DICK! They love it and they want it! The problem is they want it from the guys
they want it from. All he has to do is offer them the SECOND best thing... sexual satisfaction as opposed to sex with a man they WANT! He doesn't even have to satisfy them:) It's too late by the time he's fucking them! All he has to do is make them BELIEVE that if they get with him he is going to fuck them WELL! They couldn't resist because at some point they became HORNY and wanted that RELEASE!"

GM style lines

Nathan Szilard, ASF:

*   "If you buy me a drink, you might get lucky tonight"
*   "Well I can't please every girl but I'll give YOU a chance tonight"
*   "Women are lining up to be with me"
*   "It's tough to be such a sex symbol"
*   "Aren't you going to get too horny if I sit next to you?"
*   "I'm organising an orgy for my friend's birthday. Wanna come?"
*   "I like you because you're intelligent (gesture over her breasts). I like myself because I'm intelligent too (gesture over your dick)." (once GM even later got a phone-call where the girl said she wanted to show him her intelligence)
*   "If you're nice to me I'll lick you."
*   "How does it feel like to be with (one/two) handsome guys?"

Full Guide to Being Cocky and Funny

*   "My friend's jealous because mine is bigger."
*   "I love myself sooo much I can't leave myself alone."
*   "I wish I could split myself in 5 "me"s so that I could please ALL the women."
*   "I have to go to the hospital tomorrow" - "What for?" - "To get an operation, (pointing down) mine's too big"
*   "Do you know how I can have a 10 inch dick?" (how) "When I fold it in half"
*   "Can you help me? I have to pee and the doctor said I can't lift anything heavy."
*   "You know, if you were even HALF as gorgeous as me I'd consider sleeping with you."
*   "You're a 9.9 You'd only be a perfect 10 if you were naked and on top of me."
*   "Hey you've got something on your butt." (What?) "My eyes!"
*   "My lips are registered weapons."
*   Group approach: "Ok I'm gonna have sex with you, you, and you. Alright, who's first?"
*   "Have you tried an AUSTRALIAN kiss? It's like a French kiss but Down Under."
*   "Let's just bypass all the bullshit and let's get naked."
*   "I wonder, how would your inner thighs feel against my cheeks?"
*   "Let's flip a coin: Head at my place, tail at yours."
*   "I want to passionately kiss you on the lips...then work my way up to your bellybutton."
*   "You know, if I were you I'd have sex with me."
*   "May I pleasure you with my tongue?"
*   "It would be so good my NEIGHBOURS will have a cigarette when we're done."
*   "Your hair and my pillow are perfectly colour-coordinated."
*   "I think I could fall madly in bed with you."
*   "You look great, the only problem is your clothes." (what's wrong?) "They're still on."

Update
*   "You know, that really bothers me, all those girls going after me, and they're only interested because of it, you know...I want to be appreciated for who I am, not for just my HUGE penis."
*   "I should'nt talk about that, I don't want you to get incredibly turned on... I don't want you to make a mental picture of a huuuuuuuuuuuge throbbing tasty penis." (Nathan: "Her eyes were glowing -- you could tell what she had in mind!")

Full Guide to Being Cocky and Funny

*   "It's not possible to be cute without being picked up ... sometimes I wish I wasn't so cute" (Nathan: "One of the most important aspects of the GM technique is REVERSING ROLES")
*   You: "Do you wake up early in the morning?". Her: "No, not really". You: "Good, I don't like to be woken up".

Whenever they don't react positively enough, you say:

*   "Hide your joy / pleasure!!"
*   "Last time I saw someone as excited as you, she was in a coma!"
*   "If you don't like cute guys, just tell me!" (Most of the time the reply will be "no, no, we do like cute guys!". This question reframes their possible dislike of you into a dislike of "cute guys" in general, which however they want to deny, thus being forced to confess, that they actually do like you. Tricky eh?)

Nathan Szilard, ASF: "OKAY ONE IMPORTANT THING: you'd think that he gets blown off every time he says something that stupid, right? YES HE SHOULD!! He would IF he didn't say "JUST KIDDING " *before* she has a chance to reply. Psychologically speaking, since she does not have the time to reply negatively, she's somewhat agreeing. It's rather obvious when you see it happening. If she starts replying negatively, he cuts her down by saying, "yeah I like to say stupid things, life's too short not to have fun" or "I like to act like a little kid - I AM a kid". And then he continues with what he started with:) One other thing he uses to go kino fast and often is insulting the girl and then "apologizing" right away by kissing and hugging:)

A possible explanation of why the GM style actually works, Nathan Szilard: "You don't get rejected as you would expect - when you think about it, to reject something, you have to know what it is. When you've heard one particular line a thousand times, you know what it means, what it is, what it aims at ... When GM approaches she's here, wondering what the fuck is going on ... it's so outrageous, she can't react in a predetermined way."

From someone who tried the GM technique just to test it, ASF: "It was at the point I was feeling a little guilty because one was a real sweetheart and I just wanted to fall back to being nice and letting her talk about her boyfriend - but when I did - I could instantly see it was a mistake so I'd come off with "I gotta get an operation tomorrow..." and she'd come back with a "You're so bad" and hitting me... It was easy and she made sure to give me her phone number! I didn't even ask! This experiment tells me to memorize every one of these lines. They are killer! Pure gold! These are powerful jokes. Funny how the one who

gave me her phone number kept saying she loved a sense of humour. I thought the jokes weren't funny at all. I was just mouthing words and she was laughing. I couldn't believe it. The other one had to go but she fell right into talking about sex. WOW!'"

Update
Nathan Szilard, ASF: An idea to go beyond GM style: describing the woman as a slut. Instead of telling her "you are beautiful" as an AFC does, describe her as if she was doing something overtly and consciously sexual.

See where I'm going?

What I learned from GM, well and from textbook psychology - you can get people to form an opinion about themselves. Let that opinion be that she is a slut.

The word "slut" in this context is a highly sexual and constantly horny female (not a prostitute).

Update. Doing a pick-up on the street GM-style (suggested by Nathan Szilard, ASF). You have eye-contact with a woman on the street, she passes, and when

you turn back, make sure she hears this: "Hey! ... What does this mean? You ogle at me and you don't even stop to talk to me? I'm not a sex object!". She'll probably be standing there, looking back at you and feeling stunned, now go approach, introduce yourself, act all "hurt" for being taken as only a sex object, offer her to chance to make it up to you by having the two of you getting to know each other over a cup of coffee etc:)

Panties in the air. "Hey girls, do you know how you can tell whether you liked us?" (How?) "Well tonight, when you get back to your place, and you take off your panties, throw them in the air. If they stick to the ceiling, then that means that you liked us!" (Nathan Szilard, ASF "I couldn't fucking believe it, the girls laughed hysterically!!":)

Other GM-Style jokes:

Full Guide to Being Cocky and Funny

Q. What's the difference between light and hard? A. You can sleep with a light on.

Q. Why is sex like a bridge game?
A. You don't need a partner if you have a good hand.

It's best to use sexually overt C&F after you've already attracted the woman a bit with C&F on neutral topics, role-playing, etc. If a woman isn't attracted to you yet, and you start making all these sexual jokes, you'll come off goofy and you won't get taken very seriously. For example, imagine you're talking to a really fat chick for whom you have no attraction. You ask her what she does for a living and she says, C&F, "I'm a Victoria's Secret model". It's funny and goofy but it doesn't really arouse anything in you, since you're not attracted to her in the least to start with. You might laugh, but in your head you're thinking
"NASTY!" Now, when you first roll up on a woman, unless you're unusually attractive you're the same to her as the fat girl is to you. To her you're just another guy from the 35 who approached her so far today, and she has no attraction for you sparked in her one way or the other. If you make sexual comments at that point she might laugh, but in her head she'll think "PIG" and won't take you seriously. BUT once you get her attracted with the attraction methods, bringing up sexual themes or overtly-sexual C&F ("GM style") will get her thinking about sex. That's where you wanna be.

13. Using fluff talk to bridge between attraction points

When you meet a woman you're attracted to, at all times you should be attempting to reach "attraction points", points where her interest in you is at a peak. Getting into a fun role-play with her would be an attraction point. But the attraction point will at some point wind down (for example you can't keep a role-play up forever), and you need to keep things lively. Fluff talk is a way to keep the conversation animated between attraction points. It allows you to hold a woman's attention and interest until you find a window of opportunity to use an attraction technique or theme.

Keep your fluff talk FUN! Don't get bogged down into boring, interview-type conversation: Where did you grow up, what do you do, where did you go to high school, blah blah blah. These questions are BLAH! Every other guy will ask her these kinds of boring, unoriginal questions that bog down the fun atmosphere. You must impress upon her that you are FUN and that she should keep talking to you, so avoid "DEATH topics".

If it's not appropriate to be "fun", at least be emotionally engaging. Women see the world through their emotions, and will rarely pass up an opportunity to discuss emotions, especially relating to men & women, and dating.

If you absolutely MUST ask common questions, try and put a C&F spin on them:

"What's the story behind that?" (good for anything from a necklace to an interesting purse, etc) Ask sort of suspiciously, as if she doesn't know whether you approve of it or disapprove.

"What do you do?" (before she can answer) "Let me guess...You're a lion tamer aren't you? Do you stick your head all the way in the lion's mouth? That must be pretty dangerous work."

"What part of town are you from?" (answer) "Oh, you're one of THOSE girls?" (when she asks "what do you mean??" avoid answering and change the subject)

"So what do you do for fun?" Makes her think you might be a "fun guy" to be around, while at the same time gives you your answer as to whether she is taken or not. If she's in a serious relationship, most of the time she will mention the bf when talking about what she likes to do. You can even ask this in a mischievous way and add "Aside from the obvious stuff I mean" if the girl seems that type.

"Do you like ice cream?" (Yes) "On which part of your body do you like it best? Kidding!" Most women like ice cream and will respond to the first part of the question in the affirmative. This is also a test question to see if she's the type who'd get a kick out of GM style/sexually overt C&F. Now, if she's asking interview-type questions about you, she's interested in you and trying to build rapport. Quit the C&F after a couple questions and just
answer them from then on, and ask them back, LIKE NORMAL.

(What do you do?) "I do a lot of things." (scoff) "What, like you mean you want me to tell you where I work? Do you want to stalk me or something?

What do YOU do? Other than stalking guys at their jobs, I mean?" (blah blah, later asks again) "Guess". (Are you a X?) "Don't insult me like that! Guess again." (Second guess) "Don't insult me like that either!"

(What do you do?) "I'm a pimp, wanna be one of my hoes?" (whatever answer) "Well I couldn't take you anyway, I have a special clientele of Japanese business men who pay by the pound...so I only have really fat girls working for me. Your ass is too skinny and you wouldn't bring in enough cash."

(What do you do?) "I'm an ass model." (If she laughs stick out your ass at her, and have her hit or feel your ass to see how hard it is) "Do you dare doubt THIS ass?"

(What do you do?) "I work for a male escort agency...We specialize in G-spot orgasms. Our market research showed that women aren't having enough quality orgasms."

(What do you do?) "I'm a painter". (houses, artwork?) "FORGERIES. Van Gogh's mostly, sometimes a Picasso."

(What do you do?) "I'm one of those guys who goes around seducing rich women out of their money. Are you rich??"

(What's your name?) "Guess." ("Robert" or whatever) "Are you serious?? Do I LOOK like a Robert to you?? That's such a geeky name! That's it, there's NO WAY I'm letting you name our future kids!"

She asks you what you did today: "I went to get some things at the drugstore. You know, NEEDLES to feed my heroin habit...I was running low. But the worst part was I ran into my PIMP on the way back. He told me I wasn't bringing in enough cash, so I'd have to pull a double tomorrow night. So there goes my sleep again."

If she looks bored, here's your emergency first-aid to re-inject fun in the encounter: "You look BORED! The last time I saw a woman this excited, she was in a COMA!" (confirms she's bored) "Medic! We need 50mg of adrenaline over here, STAT!" [Place your hands apart and say] "So you're pretty sure you don't feel *this* excited yet?" (no) [Bring your hands closer] "Maybe you're feeling *this* excited?" (No, not really.) [Hold up in one hand a very small gap
between your thumb and forefinger and, smiling but seriously]: "Could you possibly be at the very least *this* excited?" If she's not smiling by now, she's a lost case. If

she IS, then say "See? You're smiling, you're starting to have fun now! So what do you do for fun when you're bored?"

If she says she's stressed: "I'll help you relax with an ancient Indian relaxation technique." (Start gently rubbing her ear lobe and pulling her hair back firmly, which of course only gets her all hot and flustered!)

If you're getting clingy vibes from her, or she seems to keep bringing up relationships: "I think that people get into relationships too fast. I think that two people should wait a MINIMUM of a few months before they even think about it. I have to know someone before I'm running around calling them my girlfriend. Most of the problems happen because people get involved too fast." Engages her in an emotional conversation, as you discuss this.

If she says she's angry about something, or it shows when she's talking about it: "Are you angry?" (a bit) "I don't believe you. I think you're FAKING anger!" (If she denies it) "Ok then, PROVE you're mad! Come on now! Show me your angriest face... GRRRRRRRRR [make a GRRRRR face] Come on, you can do it!!!" (the best part is when they TRY to put on an angry face but cant keep it) "That's a terrible mad face! I don't see a future for you in professional wrestling." This can also be used successfully as a turnaround if she's a little angry at you for whatever.

"If you really like a guy, how many times do you let the phone ringbefore you pick it up? If you only "sorta" like the guy? What if you hate the guy? Voicemail?" This can open up an interesting discussion on games she plays with guys who call her (and can even you an insight on whether she's flaky or not). It also gives material to bust on her later if she answers right away ("You answered after two rings! You must really like me.")
Last but not least, you can use the whole discussion about calling to set up a number close.

If she says she has to leave, even for a minute: "Don't tell me you were scared off by my stunning good looks and sex appeal!" This parting C&F jab will have her leave on a good note, and she'll be more inclined to come back to talk to you some more.

(Discussing some activity) "We should do that together one day...IF you BEHAVE well enough til then"

Full Guide to Being Cocky and Funny

"I BET you have a nice smile..." Right after you say that, YOU smile and wait for her reaction. "Ah! See? I knew it."

"When I find my feminine side, I won't be able to stop touching it."

"My horoscope told me I should make new friends today." (what else) "It also told me finances would be a big part of my day. Are you RICH by any chance?"

Using games

Use games as a last resort if the conversation seems to be stalling too often. Ideally you should be able to carry on a conversation for hours, and keep it interesting using the material found in this program.

Soul Gazing: "Have you ever heard of soul gazing?" (yes or no) "Really? It's something they teach in Tantra. It's where two lovers stare deeply into each others eyes to really become in touch with each other. Wanna try it?" (follow with eye contact with bedroom eyes for as long as possible, if she starts to giggle then move in and kiss her)

"Let's play the Lying Game: I ask you a question, and you have to come up with the biggest, worst LIE to answer it. The more outrageous the better! You can't just say "yes" when the answer is "no". Then you ask me a question and so on."

Groupset Fluff Talk

(For 3 sets) Use a mini cold-read by saying one is the leader, one is the shy girl that's really the bad one and one is too nice to be with the other two. If there's four, point to the fourth and say "And you, I haven't quite figured out yet." This one is good to use on your target.

(For 2 sets) Tyler Durden came up with the idea of the "Best Friends Test", and in his words, it's CHICK CRACK. They love it. Get talking with a 2-set. At a certain point say, "I'm going to test you to see if you two are close friends" (say BEST friends if they appear to be so). The girls will take you up on the challenge, and you say "Which shampoo do you use?" The two girls will ALWAYS look at each other before answering, and before they can answer you say "STOP. I don't need to hear your answer, I already know that you two are close/best friends." (How?) "Well, the first thing you did when I asked the question was, you looked at each other before answering. If you two weren't close, one or both of you would've just looked straight at me and answered right away." (In case she's joined by a male companion) "Hey, I was just asking her opinion on something and maybe both of you guys can help me on this…" Use an opinion opener. Then do a cold read on both of them. Tell the guy that he seems like he'd rather be sipping a beer, sitting on the beach somewhere, just kicking back.

"So how do you all like me so far?"

"You know what…I LOVE you guys…you guys are the best…I'm adopting you guys…you guys rock" (patronizing comment that can be applied to the whole group)

Adopt them as your rock band groupies "When I'm dirty and sweaty after a rock show, and my hair smells like smoke, you guys are gonna have to scrub me down in the shower. It's what groupies do."

"What I really need is a chick who will support me…You know, a rich girl. Are any of you rich? Do you know anyone who's rich?" (they'll name someone) "NICE… I'll be her boytoy…and then I can have affairs with you guys on the side…"

If there's a guy in the group, tease them about being lesbians and having a guy hang out with them just to have a cover. They'll laugh and insist they're not lesbians. "Too bad, cause you know that's men's #1 fantasy… What do you think women's #1 fantasy is?" (If they don't know) "I can't really tell you, I have to show you so you can experience it (move in very close to the one closest to you). It's to have adventure and danger with someone strong and powerful and it feels like THIS" (reach your hand up behind the closest girl's head and pull her hair).

14. Storytelling

Telling an interesting and humorous story about something that happened to you demonstrates value. You show that you have an interesting and fun life, as well as some interesting experiences in your past.

It's important not to brag when telling a story. You want to DISPLAY value, not parade it. If there's something in your story that could be considered of value to the girl, mention it matter-of-factly as a necessary part of the story. For example, let's say the girl tells you she's just learning to ski, and you just happen to be a ski instructor. The wrong way to go about this would be to say "I'm a ski instructor" and sit back proudly waiting for an ooh-ahh reaction. Instead, use a story to convey it in a nonchalant way. "That's cool...I remember when I started...Haha...Hey I was teaching some skiing lessons last winter and we had this 400-pound man in the group who was determined to learn how to ski...Of course he got about 10 feet down the hill before he wiped out. The guy nearly triggered an avalanche! It took 3 people to get him on the stretcher at the bottom of the hill, and when they loaded him into the ambulance...it sagged!"

When storytelling, use your voice tone, facial expressions, and body language to accentuate the story. This makes for entertaining storytelling. For example, when saying "this 400-pound man" in the story above, a good storyteller would open his eyes wide and spread has arms and say "this FOUR...HUNDRED...POUND...MAN!!"

Have 2 or 3 interesting stories off the top of your head that you can bring up at any time to liven up a conversation. Fluff talk will usually provide plenty of opportunities to segue into one of your stories, but if not, you can always use a philosophical point to transition into a story. In the case of the story above: "You know, it's funny how some people are so determined to do something that they don't realize their limitations".

15. Directing the conversation to sexual themes

The fastest way to get a woman horny is to get her talking about sex. If you tell a woman "Think about sex and get aroused" you'll most likely be either laughed at or get slapped. But by simply indulging in hot conversation you can get her juices flowing (no pun intended) and accomplish the same goal. She may even get to the point where she feels she HAS to have sex. And who will she do that with? If you've been doing a proper job attracting her with the techniques presented here, it'll be you! Even if she doesn't have intimate relations with you that very night, you've shown her that you're a sexual person who's confident about the topic. She'll also link those horny feelings to you, which will be useful for later dates.

In any interaction there'll be a proper time to turn the conversation towards sex. Often the woman will leave a wide-open window for you to comment sexually on something, and may be waiting for you to be the initiator of sex- talk (due to the ASD, "anti-slut defense"--it was YOUR fault!)

Full Guide to Being Cocky and Funny

Clifford, Clifford's Seduction Newsletter (Cliff's List): "One thing I have noticed is that a lot of women will kind of recoil when you say something a bit too sexual and then, if you pursue it with no apologies, they spring back very positively about the comment. It doesn't happen all the time, and certainly depends on the comment itself, but many women do respond to sexual comments after an initial, politically correct reaction." Once you broach the topic of sex, get into it gradually before getting into heavy stuff. Here are some things you can start off with:

1) Tell her about how your female co-workers always talk about their sex lives.

2) "Do you have any sex-crazed friends?". At some point after her answer, ask "Are YOU sex-crazed?" If she says no, "Not even a little?" If she needs a little goading into the subject, say "Awww you disappoint me!" If she's seeking your approval/wants to be liked this could entice her to get talking about sex.

Once you're successfully on the topic, fire away:

An example of a line to use in a conversation. "You need to let loose and have some FUN. When was the last time you had an orgasm? I really think you need to find a guy right now... and let him bend you over the bathroom sink and let him have his way with you."

Look for sexual innuendo in everything, and use it to accuse her of trying to seduce you before you even know her. If she says "Well, I'm getting tired, and I think it's time for bed" say "Bed? I mean, I don't even know if you know how to kiss... and you're trying to get me into bed? What happened to the old days where you could make friends first?"

"Hey I'm forming a club: --People who think of sex all day Anonymous-- Wanna join? Most meetings will probably degenerate into big orgies.....but we'll TRY to keep things under control" (if yes): "Well membership is limited, you'll have to PROVE you're worthy of membership. How horny are you?" (if no): "Well it's probably best if you don't join, we need really horny people in the group, and I don't think you'd cut it"

"If your life was a movie, what would it be rated? PG? PG-13?" (gives answer) "No X? How far away do you think you are from an X rating?" (answer) "Well, who knows? Maybe someone (subtly self-point) will jump into your life and make it an X rated movie."

"I'm not good for you. I can only promise you HOURS AND HOURS of pleasure. You need MORE than that. You need a nice guy [point to random guy] who'll give you flowers, dinners, gifts. Me, I'll just CORRUPT you."

If she mentions on the phone that she's getting all hot and bothered, say "Hey, stop trying to trick me into phone sex. I'm not that easy!"
"Wow, you wear a ring on THIS finger? You know what that says about you?"
(No) "Have you ever had sex in an elevator?" (Laughs, NO) "Well you should try it sometime!"

"Do you know what women's #1 fantasy is?" (They won't know) "I can't really tell you, I have to SHOW you so you can experience it [move in very close]. It's to have adventure and danger with someone strong and powerful and it feels like this" [reach behind her head and pull her hair]. (If she shows "goose bumps" reaction, which she should) "Oh I'm sorry, did I turn you into a quivering, horny mess?"

"What's your favorite ice cream?" (answer) "(repeat answer?) And what's your favorite part of your body to have it eaten off of?"

If she's the one to bring up sexual topics, accuse her of being a big old PERV for always having sex on her mind. Say to her: "I was trying to have an intellectual conversation, but you have to turn everything into sex! What a sinner! You're gonna burn in hell."

If she brings up the idea of sex between the two of you: "I can't sleep with you...I don't even know if you're a good kisser yet! And maybe you're a 3- minute woman, with no staying power! I need someone that lasts!"

"I love the way you spread your legs when you sit...only everything would look so much better to me if you were wearing a short dress and no panties."

"What's the craziest place you've ever had sex?" Be sure to have a damn good answer to this yourself, since she'll ask it right back.

"I don't look for one-nighters. A one night stand only means I didn't enjoy it enough to repeat it."

"Have you ever given into temptation BIGTIME? NOT necessarily in a sexual context...Unless of course you feel like answering in that context!"

If she reacts badly to taking the conversation into sexual territory: "Oh, you're a GOOD GIRL...Can I have some of your righteousness? I'm a SINNER."

Bringing out bisexuality in a woman

After a bit of sex talk you can bring up the topic of bisexuality. There are several ways to do this:

Asking: "What kind of girls do you like?" Direct and to the point. Don't fall into the trap of asking "Are you bisexual?" most women hate the label and will say no, even if they find women sexually appealing.

Joking: "So have you met any interesting guys here yet? No? Oh, so you're here to meet GIRLS then?"

Teasing: She mentions she drives a [car brand]: "I've heard that [car brand] are owned more by lesbians than any other group." (laughs if she's not a bitch) "So, are you going to get a rainbow sticker for the back?" She'll claim she's not a lesbian. "Ok good, so I won't see you at the gay parade with a shaved head and combat boots. What about just liking girls? Do you?"

Once the topic has been brought up and you're engaged in conversation about it, you can continue with this:

"I like bisexual women the most, because they're more OPEN. They're more fun, and they're better in bed. They're more adventurous, and comfortable with their own sexuality. They realize that women are sexual beings." If the woman feels she has to prove herself to you and win you over, after hearing this she'll probably drop subtle or overt hints that she's attracted to women. Once she does this, she has to follow through later to be CONGRUENT. More convincing needed? "Also, they don't get jealous if you look at other women.
In fact, they're usually the ones that notice them first! And without those jealousies in a relationship, it makes it much easier to be open and honest, to be friends as well as lovers, and to really be able to connect."

If she reveals to you that she's bisexual: "Oh, I can sympathize completely. Women are beautiful creatures, so I don't blame you for being attracted to them!" (blah blah) "You know, TECHNICALLY, I'm a lesbian!"

Ask her if she likes guys or girls more. If she admits to liking girls but says that she likes men more, say "Exactly! You like girls but you still need some deep dicking!" When you ask a girl if she's bisexual, she'll probably ask if YOU are: HER: Are you?
YOU: No.
HER: Why not?
YOU: Because it's not natural with men. For women it's natural.
HER: Explain, blah, blah.
YOU: It's yin and yang, basically. Men are YANG energy, dominant, confrontational, and two YANG energies don't mix. When you see gay couples for example, you'll never see two dominant males together. You always see either a dominant male and a feminine, submissive male, or two submissive males together. Women are YIN energy, it's a sexually nurturing energy. But in our culture it's repressed, mostly.

Sex talk in groupsets

Because of the safety-in-numbers factor, it's far easier to bring up the topic of sex with a group. Women are used to talking about sex amongst each other, and they'll be comfortable discussing it around a guy who's befriended the group. Once the topic has come up, ask blunt, bold questions for shock value. Examples:

"Ok, who sitting at this table has ever had sex with another woman?"

"Show of hands! Has anybody here had sex in an airplane? No? What about a bus? No? Geez this is one TAME bunch…Okay what about the backseat of a car? ANY form of transportation??"

"Which one of you is the easiest?"

During the discussion you may see that one of them is participating less than the others or may be acting a bit shy. Point her out with "You're not talking much. You're the GOOD GIRL of the group, aren't you? You need to find a guy to bend you over the bathroom sink and have his way with you!" Turn to her friends and say "We've gotta get this girl LAID!" If this C&F theme goes over well, continue it. Point out guys going by and whisper to her (so that everybody can hear) "Hey what about him?" etc.

"What's the difference between making love, sex, and fucking?" (blah blah blah blah, let them talk) "Here's how I see it: MAKING LOVE is this deep connection where it's more about emotion than the physical... SEX is what you do after a long hard day and you just NEED to get off, but it's no biggie... And FUCKING is raw, powerful, and feels like this (run your hand up the back of the hair of the girl closest to you, then pull her hair. She'll squirm and say something about goose bumps or whatever). Take that feeling and multiply it 100 times. That's fucking."

16. Projecting sexual state

This technique is best used after other attraction techniques. It involves adopting a sexual state, and then projecting it onto the woman. You need to OOZE sex, and have it show in the way you talk, move, and look at her. You could be talking about the weather, but your bedroom eyes, voice tone, and body language are communicating that you want her, and that you know she wants you!

The reason this works is because human beings tend to subconsciously mirror people they like. If you build rapport with her and she's having fun, she'll begin to match your state, whatever it may be. This is explained further in the section on Rapport.

17. Establishing dominance and dealing with shit-tests

Women test men for all sorts of reasons, and it's mostly an unconscious process. Attractive women have a lot of options, and prefer men who are STRONG OF CHARACTER. If you were an attractive woman being chased by hundreds of guys, how would you go about eliminating the losers? You'd TEST them, in subtle ways that test for strength and personality. If you did this on a regular enough basis, this behavior would become unconscious and automatic.
Women will ALWAYS test you! Deal with it, learn how to handle it, and move on.

The more attracted a woman is to a man, the more she'll test him. Women don't go up to 90 year-old men and say "You jerk!" and playfully punch them in the arm. They don't go up to some horribly disfigured guy in a wheelchair and say "You think you're hot shit, don't you?" They do this to the men they're attracted to! A woman is usually nice and polite with people she's not attracted to, as social conventions

dictate her to be. In fact, if a woman
is being polite and overly nice with you, it's a bad sign. But if she's testing you by calling you a jerk or an ass, it's a sign that you've aroused some interest in her, and she wants to see if it's justified.

How do you know a woman is testing you? When her lips are moving! Seriously, the way to know when a woman is testing you is to look at how whatever she's saying or doing is making you feel. Anytime her words or actions make you feel put on the spot/challenged and forced to do or say something about it, you're being tested. Any time she seems to be
attempting to take the lead ("Call me on Thursday and I'll let you know if I can accept your offer for a date on Friday"), it's probably a test.

It's important to know how to deal with feminine testing. This is one of the BASICS: Once you demonstrate to a woman that she can manipulate you, she loses all sexual attraction for you and designates you as a PAWN. You MUST retain control and be the MAN.

Most tests can be dealt with just by ignoring them. You DO NOT have to take every communication seriously and respond to it. So if a test is given (let's say she calls you a jerk), you can just smirk and go on and act as if it had never been said, and continue your conversation. The same principle can be applied when someone is getting overly emotional or dramatic with you. Continue as usual (applying humor in testing situations can be effective as well). To illustrate how ignoring a test works, here's an example of a real interaction I had with a HB and her friend in her living room. The conversation centered around how much of a player she was in clubs, and how badly she treated the guys who tried to pick her up.

OFB: (To HB) *I* could pick you up REALLY easily in a club. I have the perfect pick-up line.
HB: (in disbelief) Oh, really?
OFB: First, I'd make eye contact with you from across the room. Then I'd smile and walk over to you…
HB: Who says I'd look at you?
OFB: Then I'd look you in the eyes, and brush your hair away from your ear…
HB: HELLO, "personal space", no way I'd let you do that!
Friend: Yeah, no way.
OFB: Then I'd lean in and whisper in your ear that perfect pick-up line (LONG PAUSE,

then wicked smile as I put on my best "bedroom voice") --I HAVE
HAGEN-DAAS CARAMEL ICE CREAM IN MY FREEZER--
HB: HAHAHAHA!!! That would work! And if it was cookie-dough ice cream, I'd be at
your place before you!

Look at the dynamics of that conversation. Despite her shit-testing me 3 times
in 30 seconds (with a contribution from her friend), I just plowed through and didn't
even acknowledge her objections/tests. It worked and in the end, got a very
favorable response. By the way, this is a great routine to use with any "playerette".
Find out early in the conversation what chocolate or ice cream she's crazy about,
then eventually get onto the subject of her playing guys at clubs. Then use this
routine, plugging in her favorite sweet thing where it belongs. The beauty of this is
that she's CERTAIN to test you after your first statement, since no woman will ever
admit to being an easy pickup. And because you were the one to set up the test,
you're completely ready to ignore her shit-tests and plow through (the toughest shit-
tests are the ones that catch you off-guard).

Another way of dealing with tests is to PRE-EMPT the test! If you see her talking with
a lot of guys, say "You're such a player! Look at you." Or if she talks to you about
doing something together say "What makes you think I'd WANT to hang out with
you?" (In fact, most C&F comments are in fact tests. If you see she loses her cool,
she failed your test). The reason this is effective is that you steal the testing frame
first. When she tries to test you in retaliation, she's doing it from a position of
weakness and her tests will seem like feeble attempts to regain power...Which they
are.

Another approach: At the first sign of a shit-test, SPANK her and call her a brat. It's
not appropriate in all situations, but occasionally you can get away with it
(especially if you two are alone).

If a woman tests you by talking about other guys she's involved with, or approaches
another guy in front of you: Tell her how much you want her to be with other guys,
how humans are not supposed to be together forever, all of that. PUSH HER on
whatever guy she brings up (to try to make you jealous), and recommend that she
fuck him. If she shit-tests you back with "You don't care about me" say "I'm the only
guy you've ever met who cares ENOUGH to give you your freedom." This is called
"prescribing the symptom" -- take any behavior you don't like and tell her to DO IT
MORE.

Full Guide to Being Cocky and Funny

Shit test response: "Where'd you get that one, Cosmo or Seventeen?"

When a woman wants you to do something for her or buy her something: "OK, I'll make you a deal. I'll do X if you give me a 1 hour massage with hot oil, nice music, and candles." Remember to use a cocky/funny tone of voice, but be serious.

(I hate it when you tease me) "So why do you look at me with such pouting desire when I do it?"

Don't apologize for anything. This doesn't mean being an arse, but show that you're defying her criticism. "I don't like that shirt." "Fine, take it off me."
If a woman tries to get you back for a C&F comment: "If only you were as cute as your comeback"

(Are you a player?) "Well I like playing WITH you" (then give her a little pat on the butt, or touch her somewhere more intimate if you've already had sex)

Some more examples of shit-tests and replies:

* You bring up sex. She says "You're SUCH a perv!" You say "You're SUCH a prude! I'll bet you're an annoying good-girl."
* You make a C&F comment. She says "You're SUCH a jerk!" Reply: "You're such an EASY target!"
* You admit you like computers. She says "You're SUCH a nerd!" You say "I'm the first person you'll call when your computer crashes!"

A good example of a reply to any "You're SUCH a   " statement test is to smile and say "You LOVE me."

(You're so   ) "So THAT's why you like me so much! Ohhhh..."

Another example of an excellent comeback against a test on something about you, or a "You're SUCH a   " comment is "Awww, isn't that cute, you have an opinion!"

If she complains or doesn't like something, turn it up and give it back to her. She says "I don't like that station", you turn it up a notch and smile at her. You don't have to be an ass, you can turn it back down after. But just show that you aren't easily controlled, and are independent of what she thinks.

Always raise and call her bluff. If a woman gives you some tension or tests you, call her on it. "I'm leaving, that's it" "Ok. Don't let the door hit you ass on the way out". In most cases she wasn't planning to follow through—it was a TEST.

"Buy me a drink" Shit-Test Responses

This is a fairly common situation out on the bar and club scene. It goes like this: Woman meets guy, gets interested in him, then shit-tests him with a request for a drink to see if he'll do whatever she says.

In dealing with this, keep in mind that you do NOT owe a woman anything. NEVER open a woman at a bar, lounge, or club with "Can I buy you a drink?" It indicates that you're a supplicating man who feels he has to buy a woman's attention with material objects, and says all the wrong things in that it shows you're ASKING for her time (never ask for anything, remember). You have to keep the mindset that no matter how beautiful she may be, her looks don't get her a free ride, or a free anything for that matter. Your frame is that YOU are evaluating HER. If you're using the techniques and openers outlined in this program, you should already have proven yourself worthy of her attention without needing to buy your way into her social circle.

Sometimes a woman will ask for a drink not to test you, but just because she's greedy and wants to sucker you into buying her a free drink. In this case a refusal to buy her one will weed her out right away, so you really have nothing to lose by refusing the request.

I'm not saying it's wrong to buy a woman drinks at all times. Obviously after you've talked with her for a while and you approve of her, it's cool to call the bartender over and order for her. Do this on your own and take the lead, without prompting from her or asking on your part. Don't ask her what she wants to drink—either order another of what she's already drinking, or order some distinctive drink to show you have some culture.

Here are some responses to the "Buy me a drink" shit-test:

Her: "Will you buy me a drink?"

You: "No. But you can buy ME a drink "
Her (thinking "Argh... Gmph... He didn't supplicate! Could this be... a real man? What's this, I'm getting wet??"): "Am... um... Yes!"

OR:

Her: "Will you buy me a drink?"
You: "Give me a French kiss."
(NOTE that the tongue play must be an explicit part of the bargain up front. None of this peck on the lips BULLSHIT, because you're still supplicating if you settle for that. Here's the beautiful part: If she says no, now SHE is the person who said "no" in the situation, instead of you! You don't have to be the "jerk" for turning her down. If she says yes, tongue-action and kino/touching right away. Then get her a drink as a reward. Note that she will probably demure before caving in, and this is your chance to show personality and be playful. Go C&F on her right away!) Accessory phrases: "You aren't uptight are you? Don't you go out to have fun? We're having fun!" OR "You like cool guys don't you?"
OR "It's not HOT SEX or anything...just a little kiss!"

Her: "I need a drink"
You: "Ok, go get one, and while you're up there, grab me a rum and coke."

18. Dealing with poor behavior

Don't be shy about ejecting from a set or leaving on a date if the woman continues being a bitch or head case with no sign of letting up. If necessary, stop and step back. Excuse yourself from the set, get off the phone, or go to walk away, and say "You know, this really isn't working for me anymore. I think I'm just going to bring you home, and go relax."
Emotional Outbursts

Responding to outbursts: "So what am I going to get paid for babysitting tonight?" OR "Did this stuff work on your daddy? Why didn't he spank you more?" OR "Does acting like this ALWAYS let you get your way? Or only with the spineless guys?"
Or make fun of her silly behavior: "Awww isn't that cute, you getting all upset like that." OR "Wow you've really got this upset thing down to an art form. Does it work well with other people?" OR "Ya know, you're kinda cute when you're mad." OR "If you keep acting like a brat I'm gonna SPANK you like one."

Full Guide to Being Cocky and Funny

Flaking out

"Flaking out" is when a girl doesn't show up for a date, or gives you a bogus number. Basically it means letting you down and wasting your time.

So if hopes were high (you hit it off well, she gave you her number etc, any signals of possible interest you might have received from her will do) but now she seems to have disappeared, show that you're not cool with that behavior, and only because you saw some potential for the two of you are you willing to give her one last chance. But if she dares to do it again, its bye-bye and blam!! Door-slam time. Guys with a lot of options, or with few options who put a high value on their own time, will probably not even give a woman who pulled such crap a second chance.

The only voicemail/answering machine message you should ever leave: "Hi [girls name]. This is [my name]. I wanted to let you know how disappointed I was that you didn't call me back. But, since I saw so much potential for us I thought I would give you one last chance. So why don't you give me a call."

Some "flake prevention" ideas

1) Don't make plans too far in advance. Try not to make plans more than 24 hours in advance. Why? Because YOU'RE BUSY. If she wants your attention, she'd better be ready to accept any time you find that you can free up. And she'd better be there. Shorter time frames also make for fewer opportunities for other things to "come up". If you make plans 5 days in advance, ALL KINDS of things can come up. If you make plans 5 HOURS in advance, you have a much better chance of things happening.

2) Always talk about when you're busy before you talk about when you're available. Two to one is a good rule of thumb. "I'm busy tonight, and I can't do it Thursday. Let's get together tomorrow afternoon around 4... but I only have a couple hours, so don't be late."

3) Don't say things like "I can do it anytime" or "I'll make time for you whenever you want". This kind of thing just TELEGRAPHS the message that you're chasing her, you want her approval, etc. and that you're too AVAILABLE.

4) Give her the gift of missing you. Don't call her all the time. Don't always bug her to get together. Don't always call her back when she calls you. In other words, have your own life.

Finally, make sure she knows that it's NOT OK to be flaky with you. This takes some guts when you're dealing with an attractive woman that you like. It's not always the easiest thing to say "Wasting my time and changing plans at the last minute isn't OK with me...even if your best friend is upset tonight because her cat is having a mental breakdown." But it must be done.

If she flakes out, remember these magic words: "HOW ARE YOU GOING TO MAKE IT UP TO ME?". And as a last resort... if the problem keeps coming up with a woman, you might have to use the secret weapon:

--PROBATION--

Just say "OK, well you're now on probation. No more making plans in advance with you. If you want to see me, you can call me and ask what I'm doing right then. If I'm free, I'll see you, but you've wasted too much of my time, and I'm not going to make plans with someone who can't keep them." Then, when she asks to make plans, say on Friday, just say to her "Well, maybe. You can call me then and see if I'm free. But you're on probation now for being flaky, so no advance plans with you." Harsh? Maybe. But if YOU don't respect your own time and put value on it, then how do you expect anyone else to?

Ironically, even though these ideas might sound a little bit too extreme... and like they might scare a woman away, exactly the opposite is true. If you do these things, women will typically be MORE attracted to you, because you're acting like a MAN WHO RESPECTS HIMSELF.

If you DON'T do this stuff, she'll probably drift away from you, and you won't even realize why it's happening.

Another way to prevent flaky behavior is this: At the appropriate place and time, SHOW YOUR ANGER...In a mature way. Guys who never get mad, who never show that they will stand up for themselves and make a woman feel a bit of unpleasantness are, in effect, giving themselves away for free!! Let the females in your life know that if they break your rules, cross you, or show any lack of respect that THEY ARE GOING TO PAY A PRICE! Always look for "respect opportunities" and call women on their bullshit. Be firm and sincere. If you sense that a woman is "testing" you by being difficult, trying to change plans with you on short notice all the time, etc. then RELAX. Lean back. Never let her "get away" with anything just because she's beautiful, or let her have any "special privileges" because you like her. NEVER. When she does something you disapprove of, call her on it. Tell her that you won't put up with that shit and not to do it again. NEVER forget you were born without her. And that there are a hundreds more like her and thousands more that are even better than her.

One Tactic

YOU: Don't ever (bad behavior) again, ok? I'll always treat you respectfully, but I expect the same from you.

HER: Uh... uh... yes.

YOU: Good. Let's see you make it up to me.

And at this point grab her and kiss her passionately. If you can, try to turn this into a sex close right then and there. Why give her an evening on the town and reward her rotten behavior? You have nothing to lose at this point.

Disrespecting you can also be an extreme and immature form of testing you, if the woman likes you at first but wants to determine your worthiness or lack of worthiness. She'll be testing you in order to find out whether you are a supplicating taking-all-her-shit pussyboy or a man with self-control and the ability to take charge.

In order to pass such an extreme test (an example of which is canceling a date), you must:
1. Show that you don't lose your temper over it.

2. Show that you don't whine like a baby over it.

3. Show that it doesn't really phase you.

4. Show that you DO find it disrespectful and that you don't tolerate that.

(4) is the most important point, but you MUST do it in such a way that (1,2,3) are true!

Of course, if a woman does test you in this disrespectful way, you should seriously re-evaluate your interest in her.

Apologizing

What happens when YOU are the one who showed shitty behavior? First off, NEVER say you're sorry unless you very obviously fucked up. Move through life without apology.

If you MUST apologize to disarm a woman's negative state, make humor out of it by taking a step back, IF it's appropriate. An example of a one step forward, one step back apology: "You women are nuts!" (She gets pissed) "I'm sorry......................I'm sorry that women are nuts!!"

19. Disarming obstacles

"Obstacles" are other people who get in the way of your opening or attraction of your target. There are generally three types of possible obstacles: Your own entourage, the target's friends, and other alpha males. You must learn to deal with these obstacles skilfully while remaining cool. Doing this properly will increase attraction in your target's eyes, since she'll see that you're cool in social situations. Doing it wrong will definitely kill the attraction. If you're mean to her friends for example, they'll dissuade her from hooking up with you. And if you get blown out of the set by another guy showing you up, you'll look like a dork. Remember, in Tyler's words "the only rule of pickup is to be visibly cooler than the chick". If you don't come across properly when dealing with obstacles and don't maintain your "cool status", you'll demonstrate low social value. Obstacles are sometimes known by their slang term, "cockblocks".

Your own entourage

Unless you surround yourself with a skilled wingman or wingmen, the company you keep is a potential obstacle to your pickup and attraction efforts. Here are some situations where your pick-up can be spoiled by your own entourage:

Full Guide to Being Cocky and Funny

THE GRASS CUTTER: Cutting your grass is when a member of your entourage moves in on a woman you've opened. Once you've done the hard work of opening the target and getting her into a good state, the grasscutter will move into the set, introduce himself as your friend for social proof, and then start gaming your target. Part of his game may involve comments to cut you down, in an effort to make himself seem superior (to "out-alpha" you). ANTIDOTE: The wrong way to do it is to get in an argument with him right there. Instead, cut him out of the set using anti-AMOG tactics (described below), and don't
invite him out with you again. If you have no choice (he invites himself along or is a Siamese twin of a good friend of yours in the group), then try to ditch him and go to another part of the venue, where he won't see you opening targets.

THE THIRD WHEEL: When you move into set, a good wingman will move in and use his own material to occupy the rest of the group while you game your target. But sometimes you may be hanging out with a great, fun friend (who just happens to be lousy with women) at the time you spot your target, and he just tags along while you open them. What ends up happening is that since your buddy has no game, he just sort of hangs there boring everybody, or makes stupid comments, both of which make you look bad ("the company you keep"). ANTIDOTE: The wrong way to deal with this problem is to just let your friend
sit there, making things worse. There are several ways to deal with this. You can tell your buddy "Wait here one second", go in solo, do a quick number- close, and get out saying "I need to get back to my buddy" (In fact, having a friend waiting is sometimes a great time constraint that works in your favour). Another way to prevent the Third Wheel Effect (if your friend comes into set with you) is to constantly talk up your buddy, saying what a great guy he is, how he's crazy sometimes, etc. You're basically substituting for your friend's lack of game. Also, by inflating his sense of value, you'll put him at ease and
he may start to relax and open up. This is extra work of course, seeing as how you have to entertain the group, demonstrate value to the target, AND talk up your friend, but it beats getting blown out of the set.

THE DRUNK: Sometimes a friend who's normally cool can become a total chauvinistic ass with a few drinks in him, and threaten your game. This happened to me in Cuba several years ago. I'd been hanging out with a group of Italian guys who were cool for most of the week, but on this last night there they'd had way too much to drink. I was gaming on the cutest Cuban girl I'd seen all week outside the resort's nightclub, using teasing and flirting, and her buying temperature was high. Just when things were getting good, one of the gang starts yelling out "GO FOR IT! POUND FUCKING POUND!! NAIL HER MIKE! NAIL HER!" over and over. I tried to ignore him and keep the game on, but it was obvious that it was making her uncomfortable and she excused herself. Not knowing how to handle it at the time, I lost out. Now, The Drunk intrusion isn't necessarily only limited to cat-calls; it can also involve a drunken member of your entourage pushing his way into your set and cavemanning your target, or feeling her up inappropriately—both of which will ruin her state and kill your game. ANTIDOTE: If The Drunk intrudes, isolate your target from the group with "Let's go talk over there, there's too many drunken jerks in this spot". Physically lead her to another area, then say "There! Much quieter" and continue your conversation. OR, if she'd been grabbed, say "Ok, no one's gonna grab you over here. But I might just SPANK you if you don't behave!" (smile). Another idea, simple enough: DON'T HANG OUT WITH DRUNKS! And if you do happen to be out with some friends who eventually become drunk and rowdy, simply detach yourself from them and game targets outside of cat-call range, or preferably out of sight.

The target's friends

When gaming a set, it's important to befriend the target's friend(s). Her peers have a huge say in swaying her opinion of you, so you MUST make them like you. ENGAGE the group. Get everyone involved to avoid one or more becoming a cockblock. This means including the ugly girls of the group in the interaction too. If the y feel ignored they'll be bitter and try to sabotage your efforts, either in front of you or after you've left the set. One thing you have to be careful about is giving a non-target TOO much attention. If you talk up the ugly
girl to befriend her, the actual target may leave you two alone since she sees you hitting it off so well. Try to balance your attention so as to keep your target involved in the interaction.

Despite your best efforts to make everybody feel a whole lotta love, one thing a target's friends WILL do is test you. When they see their friend getting all doe-eyed over you and getting carried away, they may test you in her place. Some may have malicious intent in doing this, as explained above, but usually they're just looking out for their friend. You can deal with this as you do with regular tests one-on-one, but here are some specific "cockblock-destroyers":

(girl tries to pull her friend away from you) "What are you??? The drag-away friend??"

Full Guide to Being Cocky and Funny

(girl whines and complains or tests you hard) Turn to target and say "Is she always like this? How do you roll with her?" OR "Is your friend always such a brat?"

(girl bombards you with questions to put you on the spot) "You're very investigative. You're like Nancy Drew." Call her Nancy from then on!

(girl gives you a shit test, like "You dress funny" etc) Respond by completely ignoring her comment and asking her "Are you a player?" If she pouts or mouths back, call her a "Drama Queen".

(girl shit-tests you) Say "Hey, I'm talking" and then continue without responding to the shit test. Or just say "Cute" and keep going. Dismissiveness can be an effective tool.

Occasionally you'll run into a set where there are a male friend or two. A target's male friends are known as the "Beta males" (because if they were Alpha, they wouldn't just be "friends" now, would they?) If your target is attractive, odds are that the male "friend" is just there because he got the "Let's just be FRIENDS" speech. He's hanging out with her as her friend, but secretly he's still after her, and hopes by hanging around her and displaying what a great guy he is, she'll eventually come around. Because of this, the male friend is often more of a cockblock threat than the female ones. This means it's vitally important to befriend the Beta male. If you set up the frame that you're his good buddy, he'll be more reluctant to cockblock you, either on the spot or after you've left the set (since good buddies don't cockblock each other). The last thing you want is for him to see you as just some anonymous jerk trying to screw his beloved princess, and for him to feel the need to protect her from you.

Befriending him is the Good Cop approach. The opposite (but more risky) way to deal with Betas is to present yourself as the total opposite of her male friend (to whom she's not attracted). Let's say C&F is in play with your target and Mr. Beta says something like "Oh, he doesn't mean it" to the target. You say "Of course I mean it!" Treat him as you would an AMOG and blow his wimpy ass out of the set with AMOG destroyer tactics (more on these below). In general, it's good to play it safe and treat every male obstacle as an AMOG at
first anyway. Once you've ascertained that the friend is a Beta, THEN you can shift gears and befriend him. "Sorry about busting your balls earlier bro, I thought you were being rude to me but I realize now you were just looking out for your friend".

Full Guide to Being Cocky and Funny

Once you're in set with the girl and trying to isolate her: "Nice talking to you Fred, but Marie and I were just going out on the balcony to talk in private." If the Beta starts following you around like a lost puppy, say (nicely) "Hey Fred, looks like we need to get you hooked up with one of the girls here at the party so you don't have to follow us around. Anyone spark your interest?"

Other alpha males (AMOGs)

One thing you'll eventually have to contend with while picking up is the Alpha- Male, Other Guy (AMOG). The AMOG is basically your competition. Someone with decent game, looks, money, muscles, etc. or any combination of these. In other words, someone who's a potential threat to your success with the target.

A note on fighting

Don't worry about it. Unless you're in a biker bar or some Tijuana shithole, the odds are miniscule that an AMOG will fight you over a girl. Usually deflating him using AMOG destroyers will be enough to blow him out of the set and leave you alone. Losing his cool and fighting you over her will just make him look bad in her eyes and worsen his already bleak chances, and he knows it. In fact, most people will go to great lengths to avoid a fight. Not only do they run the risk of getting their asses kicked or badly injured, they also risk getting roughed up by the bouncers throwing them out, spending a night in jail, sitting in court, the stigma of a criminal record, and maybe even prison time or a fine.

There are two exceptions to this though: The first is the mean drunk. A mean drunk is usually extremely short-sighted and won't care how stupid he looks in front of the target. All he'll care about is kicking your ass for moving in on "his" girl (even though chances are he acted like an idiot anyway while he engaged her). The best thing to do when a drunk is involved is to NOT use AMOG destroyers on him. Instead, wait until he blows it and/or the girl gets fed up of his constant pawing and beer breath. Once he walks away (or gets carried away by club security), move in and feel free to use the situation as part of
your opener. Something like "That guy was grabbing you everywhere! Don't you feel like you need a shower now?"

The other exception is the criminal kingpin. The big drug dealers, gang members, and mobsters tend to like their women hot. So if you make a habit of approaching and flirting with hot women, you run the risk of eventually gaming one of their "trophies" at some point. The good news is that these types go to great lengths to avoid run-ins with the law, so they won't do anything rash (like have you crippled or shot) when they see you talking with their girl. What they'll do is have someone (or several someones) come up to you and give you a fair warning. Do yourself a favor and heed it; there are plenty of other women in the world you don't have to risk your health for. You might think this would never happen to you, but I was in a situation a couple years ago where I made contact with a STUNNING Venezuelan woman on the Internet. She was a hostess at Montreal's most popular strip club, which happened to be part- owned by a Montreal mob figure's son...who happened to have been involved with her until just before we met, I eventually found out. She kept inviting me to come meet her at the club when the guy wasn't around, but no way was I getting involved there. The last thing I needed was a connected family member coming in and seeing me gaming his recent ex-girlfriend. If you find yourself in a similar situation, consider the possible consequences and do the smart thing.

Anti-AMOG Tactics

Tactic #1:

The quickest and cleanest way to blow an AMOG out of a set is to pelt him with friendly, logical, interview-type questions to make him look BORING. Here's how it works: The Alpha male comes into the set, all confident and cocky and funny. He's using teasing, flirting, funny stories, and other tools to get her attracted. The girl gets into state. Then YOU show up, and start asking him "Hey bro, so where are you from?" "Oh cool, how'd you get downtown?" "Oh, what kind of car do you drive?" "That's a nice car. Did you have trouble finding parking?" ETC ETC ETC. Eventually the target falls out of state, since everything coming out of the guy's mouth is now BORING, logical answers, the kind of stuff that doesn't get her revved up emotionally. She's now a clean slate, and all the AMOG's work to get her into state is ruined. To top it off, now YOU are the dominant male, because you're controlling the conversation (even if only by asking boring questions), and he's following your lead. He realizes he's lost control of the situation and there's no point in him sticking around.

The logical questions approach is pure genius. Not only do you blow out the AMOG, but you do it in a friendly way. All you really did was ask him friendly questions about himself, so it avoids any confrontation that may have resulted from challenging him.

Tactic #2:

In cases where the AMOG is more challenging (won't let you into the set, won't let you engage him in logical questioning, is condescending to you, etc.), you have to take a harder line. With this type you have to be a little patronizing. As you do with comments to women that make them self-conscious, make the AMOG feel self-conscious and deflated about things that he really shouldn't feel self-conscious about in the first place. Clothing is an easy target:

"Oh man, you're wearing a (BRAND NAME) shirt? You're sooo cool, dude." His likely response will be "What? What's wrong with (BRAND NAME)?" Come back with "Nothing dude! In high school I used to wear (BRAND NAME). It's all good".

"Wow dude, that's a nice (shirt/watch/suit/hat/scarf). I bet you get ALL the girls with that."

"I love that shirt man! Abercrombie rocks. I used to wear that shit in high school all the time!"
ATOM BOMB: "That's a wicked shirt. Where can I get one like it?" (answers with store) "(Store)? Awesome. You're like my PERSONAL FASHION ASSISTANT, dude! Keep the good advice coming! Like Queer Eye for the Straight Guy!"

You can also use the AMOG's personal style, be it hair, jewelry, or posture, to make him self-conscious:

"Dude, that's such a nice big gold chain! Is it real?"

For Gino types: "I like your style, bro! You're like an Italian Stallion!"

"Bro, your hair looks great. How much gel did it take to get it like that?"

For rappers: "I like your style, bro! You look like 50 Cent/P Diddy in that video." (depending on which one his clothing resembles most).

For white rapper wannabes: "I like that style you've got going, dude. Eminem's

Full Guide to Being Cocky and Funny

wicked!"

For new wave guys: "Awesome style dude, the hipster look fucking rocks!"

For preps: "Dude, you're dressed to the 9s! You're overdressed for this place." Another factor that can be used to make an AMOG self-conscious is their location or school:

"You guys are from St-Leonard? You guys are sooo cool! Shit, you know I gotta impress you St-Leo guys."

"You go to McGill? Dude, you're sooo cool! McGill is SUCH an awesome school!"

Misc Tactics:

If you're on the dance floor, and he's a mediocre dancer: "Man, you're such a great dancer! Show me some of your moves."

"Man, you and that girl make SUCH a great couple! You should marry her. Go ahead, propose to her!" To avoid looking like he's not playful, he'll likely mock-propose to the target and look like a dork, as anyone proposing to a girl they just met would look. Then say "Actually, you know what? You two look too much alike, almost like brother and sister. That's like incest! (Turn to target) Like marrying your own brother!" The association will be made and she'll lose attraction for him at the thought of "getting involved with her own brother".

"Hey bro, these are my little sisters. They just broke up with their boyfriends! Talk to them. Bro, they're *feisty*. I'll give you two hundred dollars to take them off my hands!"

AMOG makes a smartass comment to you: "What? What did you say? No, man, what did you just say to try to make yourself look cooler than me? Come on, man, I wanna hear this!"

After talking for a bit with the logical Q&A tactic: "You know, I thought you were a TOTAL prick at first, but you're pretty cool! You should come to (PLACE) this weekend and meet my friends."

Full Guide to Being Cocky and Funny

The key is to say these things with a BIT of sarcasm in your voice, and to exaggerate your enthusiasm slightly. By doing this you make the AMOG feel self-conscious about what you were commenting on. He can't really say anything, because for all he knows you may have been paying him a sincere compliment!

Demonstrate total confidence that the girl is yours. Do it with a smile and a wink rather than a grunt and a scowl. Don't be territorial or angry, but show her that you're going after what you know you want. She'll appreciate the take-charge attitude.

If for some reason the AMOG gets angry, say "I'm joking around, man. I'm not fucking with you. What's up man?" Generally the AMOG will befriend you, because they feel the emotional/psychological heat of the interaction, and they want relief of that discomfort. They wanted a return to their comfort zone, which you gave to them.

If you happen to be out with a wingman, another tactic you could use is to have him handle the AMOG. Have him engage him, bombard him with logical questions, and position himself between him and you. Have him get uncomfortably close to the AMOG while he's talking so he backs up. By the time you close your target your wingman will have pushed the AMOG to the other side of the room. The larger/taller/more built your wingman is, the better he'll be able to accomplish this.

Finally, the quickest thing you can do to indicate superiority over a guy is to pat him on the shoulder while you're speaking. In a group, pick the ringleader and do it to him while you're saying something funny. This will help put you not only above him, but also his boys. Watch out though, unless your completely congruent with this and also use total alpha attitude, you may piss guys off, especially if their alpha themselves.

AMOG advances when you're on a date

What's the best thing to do when you're out on a date and a guy is making his move on your girl? The best thing you can do in one of these situations is what you do BEFORE it ever happens... and it's a combination of things:

1) Realize that there's nothing to be insecure and jealous about, and that these things only lead to fear and loss.

Full Guide to Being Cocky and Funny

2) Get your game in shape with women. Get yourself to the point where you can meet women in ANY situation, this way you always know DEEP DOWN that if any woman you're with ever decides to leave, you can turn around and start meeting women. This eliminates insecurity.

3) Mentally prepare. Take some time to imagine that you're in one of these situations, and notice the feelings you have. Go over it in your mind until you can think about it without having any negative emotions triggered.

And here's what to do when you're actually IN the situation:

1) EXPECT IT. If you start dating hot women, other men will hit on them, GUARANTEED. It's part of life. You have to expect that it's going to happen, and not be surprised when it does.

2) Learn how to have FUN with it. Most guys have no game at all... and it's kind of funny to watch and listen to them. Start to enjoy watching guys try to meet women, because they FAIL miserably in most cases. Wait until a guy is finished trying to pick up on the girl you're with, and then get her to share the details so you can laugh.

3) Suggest that she date the guy. Say "Hey, you guys would make a cute couple... I think you should go for him." Of course, this is all said in a light, fun way.

4) Get her laughing and in a good state, then throw her over your shoulder and walk away from the guy (smirking back in his direction optional!)

5) If you suspect that the girl you're with is actually TRYING to make you jealous, talk to other women. If you actually think that a woman is deliberately trying to make you jealous, you must do some thinking as well. Some women enjoy making men compete over them, and you probably don't want to be with one of these women. They're a pain. But if you think it's just a typical situation and the girl is trying to figure out if you "really" like her (because you'll get jealous if you do), then just turn around and start a conversation with a group of girls... and wait for her to come and find you.

Usually, if a woman is on a date with you and has any respect for you at all, within 30 seconds she'll have blown out the guy making advances on her. If she hasn't, then you really should consider whether you should be out with her in the first place.

If a group of AMOGs is blatantly cat-calling your girl from across the street, construction site, etc: Yell out to them "Thanks guys, but I'm taken!"

Generally, AMOG battles don't last that long—usually a few seconds at most. Most guys are already under stress just talking to a hot woman. Even though they may appear cool on the outside, their confidence is hanging by a very thin thread. It doesn't take much for you to move in and use anti-AMOG tactics to upset that delicate balance and blow them out. In fact, often anti-AMOG tactics won't be needed; when the guy sees you move in and start talking to the girl, and the things you're saying and doing have her smiling and laughing, he'll feel defeated and excuse himself from the set.

20. Dealing with Let's Just Be Friends (LJBF)

If you've done a lousy job of attracting a woman, or maybe you did great for a while and then slacked off and got boring, you'll probably hear this suggestion from her sooner or later: "Let's just be friends".

If a girl ever blocks advancing the relationship by popping that dreaded phrase, say "No thanks, I have enough friends." By continuing this type of relationship, you portray yourself as someone who has nothing better to do than hang around with a girl who is not that interested in you. The relationship will never get to where you want to go—to bed for some romance, passion, and sex.

A flattering rejection of her offer: "I don't view you as a friend. I view you as a woman - a very sensual and intelligent woman. And I won't apologize for that. If you're gonna make me another one of your girlfriends, I'm not interested".

If you walk away from such a relationship, you've established that you're the type used to leading a relationship, you have plenty of other girls willing to take you on your terms, and she's losing out. Often a man will completely turn around the relationship as soon as a girl sees that he's willing to "walk" rather than accept something that's not on his terms.

When do you give up on a girl? When do you decide that a relationship isn't advancing? When you're the only one making an effort to keep it advancing. If she is not putting energy in to you, take the hint and move on to the next prospect. Don't stay where you're not appreciated. If this situation does occur, try to figure out why. How did she perceive you? What turned her off? Learn from your mistakes.

Another tactic, if you can see that you're approaching LJBF-land with a girl: Completely and totally cut off all contact with her for a few months. When you come back, you can almost start from scratch. You'll be more of a stranger, and less of a "close friend".

If you decide to keep her as a friend, make sure it's on YOUR terms. Tell her that you're going to treat her like one of the fellas, that she's gonna help you meet women, and that you're going to meet other women in front of her. If she refuses, say: "Ok, fine... but I offered you my time sexually, then I offered you my time NON-sexually... you just turned down BOTH... WHAT DID YOU WANT TO MEET ME FOR?"

"FINE...then be a good FRIEND and hook me up with some of your horny friends."

21. Advancing to Qualifying Her

At what point do you decide that it's time to advance the interaction, and phase-shift to qualifying her? A good rule of thumb is to advance once you've received THREE positive indicators of interest (IOIs). An IOI can be anything that signals attraction, like a shit-test, touching you, lingering eye contact, positive statements of intent (SOI), that doggie dinner-bowl look (DDB), advancing role-plays on her own, qualifying herself to you, primping, etc.

Most of the time it'll be pretty obvious, through body language/touching, tonality, and mannerisms, that she's attracted to you. If you've REALLY done a good job attracting her, she'll actually be at the point where she's the one chasing YOU. This is called the HOOK POINT.

Chapter 4

QUALIFY PHASE

1. The purpose of qualifying
2. Implicit Qualifying
3. Indirect Qualifying
4. Cocky & Funny Qualifying
5. Direct Qualifying
6. Phase-shifting to RAPPORT

1. The Purpose of Qualifying

The process of QUALIFYING conveys that you're the selector without saying it outright. It basically shows that you hold standards and expectations of women you get involved with, and sows seeds of doubt in her mind about whether she "qualifies" to be with you. This is beneficial because it sets up that you're a challenge, and that SHE has to prove herself to YOU.

Most men follow the opposite strategy, and try as hard as they can to prove themselves to the woman. They brag about their accomplishments, their educations, or their jobs, they ask what she likes in a guy and then say "Oh, I'm like that" and give examples, etc. They look for her approval in their statements, like when saying something and following it up with "right?" or "Don't you agree?" They say things like "Give me a chance, you won't regret it" or "What have you got to lose by going out with me?" They compare themselves to her other options, saying crap like "Oh I'll treat you better than those other guys". They do everything possible to show that they're "good enough" for her.

When a man does these things for a woman, what does all that communicate? It communicates that SHE is the prize, the one with higher social value, and that he's trying to prove his social value to HER. Social-proofing yourself (bragging or trying to prove your worth) is ALWAYS a bad move for this reason. Remember, the key to pick-up is to prove that you are cooler than the girl. If you're the one trying to prove your social worth to her it sets her up as being cooler than you, and you fail.

Qualifying is extremely powerful because it implicitly puts YOU in the frame of the selector, and her in the frame of the selectee. Most beautiful women will have never seen this in their entire lives, so when a man comes along and steals her selector frame she's totally unprepared for it. If you assert the frame powerfully she won't have any choice but to be drawn into it by default, and she'll find herself trying to qualify herself to you.

Another benefit is that by getting her to worry if she's good enough for YOU, she won't have time to worry about whether you're good enough for HER.

The first step in being good at qualifying women is to have STANDARDS (this is covered in the first phase, ATTITUDE). KNOW what you want in a woman's appearance and personality, and make it clear to yourself. Then when you meet a woman you'll be in a much better position to qualify her to see if she meets your standards. The trouble with most men is that the only clear standard they hold is that they want a beautiful woman. When they can see right away that a woman's beautiful, they're SOLD, and they have nothing else to qualify her against. SHE then becomes the selector because they've already been sold on the goods. The truth is that out of every 10 women attractive enough to catch your eye, only 1 or 2 will actually be good matches for you sexually, in a relationship, or as friends. So learn to look at beauty as only one standard out of many.

There are three important rules to qualifying:

1. The most important thing about qualifying is that you do it only AFTER you've attracted her. If she's not that interested in you and you say something like "I prefer ADVENTUROUS women. Are you adventurous?" she might be a shy girl and think "Ok, I'm not what he's looking for", and she'll lose interest and slot you in the friends category in her head. But if you've already got her hella interested in you and attracted, THEN you say something like that, she'll try to prove herself to you by talking about the time she went parasailing on vacation, or that time she got up in front of everybody and danced on the speaker, etc.

2. Unless you've already completely ruled out the woman as a potential (like she's fat but you only date skinny women), the best qualifying statements

Full Guide to Being Cocky and Funny

ALWAYS leave the woman a way to qualify herself. If she's a blonde, don't say something like "I don't like blondes", because she can't do much about that. But if you say "I like women who are fun to be around and joke a lot", she can start telling jokes and being more animated to win your approval. As much as possible, keep your qualifying statements a little ambiguous. Saying "I prefer women with IQs over 140" will automatically shoot her down if she tested at 128. But saying "I prefer smart women who can hold an intellectual conversation" gives her a way to start bringing up deeper conversation topics that show her intellect.

Once you have your standards nailed down, you've got the green light to begin qualifying women. There are several ways to do this.

2. Implicit Qualifying

Implicit qualifying involves showing approval after the fact (after she says or does something). It implies that you're evaluating her. It usually comes as a surprise to a woman, because she probably had no idea you were even sizing her up until you said it; she probably thought in her mind that it was HER doing the qualifying.

* "You seem cool. I think we may end up really liking each other." "SEEM", "MAY". Talking like this subcommunicates that you're evaluating her according to your standards, and you haven't decided yet. She still has to prove herself to you.

* START TO USE THE "POINTS" SYSTEM AS SOON AS POSSIBLE! Steal the frame by saying, every time she demonstrates behavior or says something you approve of, "Wow, you're scoring points with me" or "100 points for that one". How many times have you heard this statement from a woman? This turns the game around on the woman and signals that YOU are the qualifier.

* "So many people are so judgmental about things. You seem really open and fun".

* (Says something stupid) Reply C&F: "How can you say that? I was just starting to like you."

* "You know, maybe I was wrong about you. At first I thought you were, but now I see that you're actually   . That's cool."

Another form of implicit qualifying is through body language. For example, you could fold your arms and then ask an innocent question in a slightly suspicious tone, while maintaining powerful eye contact. Even though the question you asked may be innocuous, the manner in which you asked it will get her thinking that you're carefully evaluating/qualifying her answer.

3. Indirect Qualifying

Indirect qualifying involves talking about women in general terms, and not directing the qualifying process directly at her. You're stating your standards matter-of-factly and not targeting HER specifically, but in her head she's wondering if SHE measures up to them. Here are some examples:

*   You get on the subject of dating, and you say "You know, I find it funny when women think all they need to impress me is LOOKS. Just once I'd like to meet a pretty girl with a friendly, cool personality too."

*   "I'm just sick of it you know, girls have NOTHING to say. They think that just because they look good that's enough... But it's NOT! You know, beauty is common in this city, but what's rare is a great personality. A great personality can really make dealing with someone more interesting."

*   "I want a woman who really EXCITES ME. I don't want to get involved with someone unless they really blow me away. Before I give my time and energy to anyone they've got to PROVE TO ME that they have some great qualities. And, if someone can do that I'll give it back to them in spades. I'll give them experiences that most women only get to fantasize about because I can appreciate a good thing when I see it."

*   If you've talked about the topic of sex, here's an indirect sexual qualifying statement: "A lot of women out there LOOK good, but the sad fact is they're LOUSY in bed. They never had a reason to be good in bed, because guys will still want to sleep with them based on their looks. A woman who not only LOOKS good, but can make my toes curl in bed, is
the kind of woman I'm looking for."

4. Cocky and Funny Qualifying

C&F is great for qualifying, because a woman might not know if you're joking or not.

138

www.SeductionFiles.com

* Lean back and look at her analytically, without saying anything. When she says "What?? What is it?", pause a second then say "I'm still trying to figure out if I really like you or not." Then smile like a sly devil.

* "I can tell you're a woman with great taste." (How do you know?) "Because you laugh at my jokes!" (laughs) "See? Just like that!"

* "Are you rich? I need a rich woman to support me. No? Okay do you have cable? Great! So I can watch afternoon soaps."

* "Are you a BAD girl?? Yeah right, whatever...You're like "PG13" bad...You can't hang with me unless you're FOR REAL...Are you adventurous?" (yes) "Are you spontaneous?" (yes) "Good, because I can't hang out with someone who isn't spontaneous. What's the most adventurous thing you've ever done? Really, you did X-ACTIVITY?? hmm...OK MAYBE you're cool..."

* "We could never be together, because I wouldn't take your shit, and you wouldn't take MY shit. We'd fight all the time... and I'D WIN".

* "How old are you?" (tells age) "(repeat age)??? I thought you were at least (add 5 years to number she gave). That's okay though, I can handle older women!"

* (when she does something you dont like) "Well, its just not working out between us. No more sex for you, no more kisses, no more cuddling, until you're a good girl!"

* "To me, a girl has to be honest. She has to be smart and flirty and playful and fun. She has to have good friends and family that she loves so she's not needy. And she has to be able to fix cars and pay my bills. Can you fix cars?" (No) "Well, you have the cutest little (accent/voice/sense of style) so I'll keep talking to you anyway."

* "You know, you're pretty cool. I could actually get to like you. But don't get any ideas, cause I'm not that easy."

5. Direct Qualifying

Direct qualifying makes it clear to the woman: You're seeing if she's good enough to be with you. Direct qualifying is often heavily shit-tested. If you find yourself being shit-tested on it, ignore the shit-test and just repeat the initial qualifying statement, to show that you mean business.

* "Are you in any kind of therapy? I don't like dating women with too many emotional problems." This approach to qualifying is a little strong, and it's akin to a woman asking a man straight out "How much money is in your bank account??" But it's direct and to the point, and weeds out problem women fast. If you're going to use it, smile as you say it and ask it in a matter-of-fact way.

* "Quick…Name 3 things about yourself that you think are attractive that have NOTHING to do with your physical appearance."

* "Yeah you're hot, but one thing I've learned from living in Montreal…is that beauty is common…but people with a great energy…and a great attitude…and a great outlook on life are rare…and they're worth working to get to know better… What's YOUR outlook on life?"

* "I'm not sure if you could handle me…Most women can't handle me. They fall in love and then turn needy. And I can't stand women who're needy."

* If a woman constantly shit-tests you: "One thing I don't tolerate is drama…You seem like you might be drama, so I'm not sure you're gonna make the cut". If she shit-tests you on that, come back with "See? More drama. You just can't be laid back and take things easy."

* "You could never be my girlfriend. I think you're just too sweet for me. Then again, the sweet ones are the keepers."

* Complains that she can't find a man: "What's wrong with you, that nobody's asking you out?"

* "You know what? I have to ask you, were you ever a fat girl in high school? Because fat girls develop the best personality. You have a fat girl personality."

One great thing about qualifying a woman is that once you qualify her and she meets the standards, she then has to be CONGRUENT to those standards. If you ask her "Are you spontaneous and adventurous?" and she answers yes, then when you move in to kiss her she gets all shy and pulls away, you can point out the inconsistencies in her behavior. "I thought you were spontaneous and adventurous!" She has no choice but to admit she was bullshitting (and fail to qualify), or to follow through.

Keep in mind that the qualifying statements above are just examples. Once you've decided on your standards and what you want in a woman, come up with your own implicit, indirect, C&F, and direct qualifying statements for each quality.

6. Phase-shifting to RAPPORT

It's important not to overdo the qualifying phase. Sometimes just a simple phrase like "You SEEM cool" will be enough to get the message across that you're the one doing the choosing. Especially in a street pickup situation where you don't have much time, you don't want to waste too much time on qualifying when you're better off building attraction and rapport as much as you can. As soon as you've issued a qualifying statement (perhaps two for stuck-up women), watch for rapport-seeking cues from the woman, then move
on to the Rapport phase.

Chapter 5...

RAPPORT

1. Establishing the Conversational Framework
2. Active Listening
3. Showing Empathy
4. Captioning
5. Using her Trance Words
6. Verbally Pacing her Reality
7. Demonstrating Cool Vulnerability
8. Using Indirect Complements
9. Dealing with Awkward Silences
10. Using Cold Reading Techniques
11. Matching and Mirroring
12. Potential Problems in Rapport-Building
13. Phase-Shifting to Amplify

After opening, attracting, and qualifying the girl, the next step is to developRAPPORT with her.

Rapport is a sense of connection and understanding with another person. This connection comes from a bond of commonality. In other words, when people are like each other, they tend to LIKE each other.

Developing rapport in a pick-up or seduction is important. If all you do is just attract and qualify a woman, she'll like you, but she won't feel a connection to you. As soon as you're not around she'll go out of state and the effect you created will drop back to zero. If you want a LASTING connection, or enough of one that she remembers you when you call, you need to develop some rapport. You want the woman to be thinking "He's just like me" or "We have so much in common" or "He understands me". Also, rapport builds COMFORT. Comfort is essential to getting a woman to give you her phone number, a kiss, or a wild
night of furniture-destroying sex. A woman generally needs to feel comfortable with you (at different levels of course) before she'll do any of these things.

Full Guide to Being Cocky and Funny

Guys who have trouble getting women are usually very good at building rapport, but not very good at generating attraction. "Nice guys" and their rapport-building expertise are good at instilling COMFORT in a woman, and that's why she views them as "just friends". They're all comfort, no attraction.

In basic terms: All rapport + no attraction gets you slotted in the "friends" category. All attraction + no rapport gets you slotted in the "lover" or "one- night stand" category (IF the woman even has that category at all; she may NEED rapport before having sex). Or if you're in a bar or club she may just see her being into you as a "club thing". A combination of both attraction + rapport has the woman seeing you as a potential boyfriend, which gives you more power and more options on where you want to take things. Therefore I personally recommend that guys build at least a small level of rapport with a woman they're interested in—after attracting her.

NOTE: Whatever technique you use to establish rapport with a woman, it must be SINCERE. Don't try to bullshit a woman into feeling rapport with you, because she'll be likely to pick up that you're insincere. You must have SOME sort of belief in what you're saying. Don't say "Hey I love country music too!" if listening to it makes you homicidal; just dig further and look for something else to connect on!

When do you move into the Rapport phase? When she starts asking rapport- seeking questions about you, like "What do you do?" "What kind of music do you like?" etc. When you start to hear these questions, don't go directly into rapport-building just yet. Wait a bit! If you go right into it you give her what she wants and reduce the challenge. If she asks you what you do for example, stall for a bit with C&F: "I'm an ass model." Her: Be serious! "Okay, I work in the slave trade business, you know, import/export." Her: Tell me! "Ok, ok, you've been through enough teasing...for now. I work in (insert real job here)." With certain techniques like cold-reading and indirect compliments (described below), you don't need to wait for her to take the initiative, and you can use these to start rapport building without her lead. (The Rapport phase is the exception to the rule that the man must always lead. If you lead in trying to establish rapport, it shows too much interest in her. Better that you wait until she attempts to build rapport with you instead, or use an indirect approach like cold reads or mirroring).

1. Establishing the Conversational Framework

Full Guide to Being Cocky and Funny

Rapport-building will take place in the context of conversation—at first. And within that conversation, two people who are just meeting each other will be asking questions to seek out some common ground for that connection. Here's an example:

Guy: What are you studying in school?
Girl: Philosophy. I'm 2nd year right now.
Guy: Interesting, I just finished reading Walden yesterday. What do you think of Thoreau?

Connection made, common ground found, some rapport established. It can be over anything; connections can be made on the type of music you listen to, or even what brand of potato chips you like best.

Guy: What kind of music you like?
Girl: I listen to hip hop, Ja rule, Sean Paul, all that.
Guy: Sean Paul is da shit! You see the video he just came out with?

The more complex the thing that two people have in common, the more potential there is for rapport in discussing it. Obviously the potato chip example above might give you a connection, but there's nowhere to really go with it—unless you're both huge potato chip fans, or both work for Frito-Lay, etc.

Questions that aim to search for a connection are known as "emotional bids". Here are some common examples:

"What do you do?"
"What kind of music/movies/novels/TV shows/food do you like?" "What are your hobbies?"
"What do you do for fun?" "What are your roots?"
"What part of town do you live in?" "Where did you grow up?"
"What high school did you go to?"

These are the most common rapport questions you hear being used, but they aren't necessarily all that great. The reason is that they're CLOSE-ENDED questions. If you ask "Where was your last vacation?" and she says "Hawaii", you don't have much to use for a connection if you don't know anything about the Hawaiian Islands. Once she answers, the question is "closed" and you have to "open" another question.

Full Guide to Being Cocky and Funny

Always aim for long answers—they're better than short ones. They give you more information to find out if you have anything in common. To get a long answer, you have to ask an OPEN-ENDED question. For example:

Guy: Where was your last vacation, and what made it great?
Girl: I was in Hawaii. The really great part about it was that I learned to surf! I also went tandem skydiving over the big island. It was beautiful.

In this example, even though you're clueless about Hawaii you've also found out that she learned to surf and went skydiving. If you know anything about either activity, or something related (let's say you were into windsurfing in your teens), you've got your "in" to make a connection. The more information she gives you, the more likely it is that you'll find some common ground.
Here are a few other open-ended questions:

"Tell me more about yourself."
"How do your friends describe you?"
(She describes an event) "How did that make you feel?"
(She describes a situation) "Have you ever been in that situation before?"
(She mentions an experience) "What was that like?"
"What do you find is really challenging about your work (school)?"

"Shy" women are often just regular girls who need a good amount of rapport established before they can open up and be themselves. Open-ended questions are great tools for getting the information out of shy women and building that connection so that they can relax around you.

Whenever asking rapport-building questions, have a subtext of approval in your communications. Asking "Why did you become a nurse?" could be construed as a negative, "Why the hell did you become a nurse?" Especially if you were teasing her earlier and going cocky & funny. Instead, ask "What INSPIRED/ENCOURAGED you to become a nurse?"

A great question to develop DEEP rapport: "What are you passionate about? What turns you on?" If she starts talking about sex, set up a booty call. If she talks about her job, art, whatever, use that to build more comfort.

While conducting rapport-building conversation, there are two elements you have to be aware of:

1) Hooks: Hooks are points of interest to feed on. If you see her getting really excited when you mention a TV show for example, go in that direction.

2) Red Flags: Red Flags are subjects to avoid. If you bring a topic up and she rolls her eyes or starts to act closed off, then you've discovered something that doesn't engage her.

2. Active Listening

Once engaged in conversation, just listening is not enough. You have to PROVE you're listening to her. Here are two ways to do this:

1) Listen with a blank, still look: Don't react to what she is saying until she's done. React to what's said in the full context of the message. Don't nod and go "Yeah, uh huh, I see" while she's talking because that comes across as blindly agreeing and also that you aren't even listening.

2) Amplify her reactions: Whatever reaction she has to something, repeat it back to her in a way that demonstrates an understanding of it. If it's a negative reaction, try to put a positive spin on it.

3) Echo her words: If she says, "Yeah, it was a tough exam session and I pulled a lot of all-nighters, but I survived" say "Yeah, you survived. It's over now." You repeat the main point of her last sentence, with different wording.

3. Showing Empathy

Empathy is a way of saying "I understand how you feel". This isn't a good way to say it though, because maybe you have absolutely NO CLUE how it feels to be groped by that guy over there in the club, or to have your dress ripped up getting out of the limo on grad night, or whatever it was that she was trying to relate. A safer and subtler method is to say things like:

"That must've been hard"
"I'll bet you were happy" "I'm sure you were excited"
"You were annoyed, I'm sure"

"You were probably sooo embarrassed!"

Another way to show empathy with her is to label her emotions. This is done by labeling her current state and communications with a feeling:

"You sound excited" "You sound tormented"
"You seem pretty broken up about it" "Wow, you're really passionate about…"
"I've never met someone so intense about this"

4. Captioning

Captioning means excerpting a phrase from a story or experience they related to you and feeding it back later. When the girl is telling a story, pick up on some part of it that she's obviously proud of. Then, refer to it later on in the conversation.

For example, let's say she's a teacher and she tells you a story about how the power went out in a classroom with no windows, and how she managed to get all the 1st graders out safely into the hallway. Later, when you're talking about her organizational skills, you say "Well if you can get 30 scared children out of a dark room with no problems, I'm sure organizing things is no problem at all for you!" Inside jokes are also forms of captioning. Anyone else hearing the joke won't understand it because they don't have the connection you two have.

ONLY caption events that she's proud of. Don't tease her about embarrassing moments or be condescending to her accomplishments unless you're trying to BREAK rapport (more on this in the AMPLIFY section).

5. Using her Trance Words

During a conversation you'll find a woman leaning on certain words. Watch for these, because this means that these words have impact to her. Imagine she says "I had such a FANTASTIC time at Virginia Beach last summer! I can't describe to you how FANTASTIC it was down there." Obviously the word "fantastic" is one of her "trance words".

When you detect trance words, feed them back to her in your communication. Instead of saying how much fun you had in Florida around the same time, tell her what a fantastic experience it was. In other words, you'll be "speaking her language".

Be careful to use the exact trance words as she says them. If she tells you her uncle has a MAGNIFICENT home, and you say "You're right, it's a FANTASTIC home", it misses the point entirely. Her trance word is "magnificent", and the word "fantastic" probably doesn't have the same impact to her. If you remember the Seinfeld episode where Elaine's love interest calls the ugly baby "breathtaking", then you understand how this works!

6. Verbally Pacing her Reality

By verbalizing her current situation, you make it more acceptable to her and she finds herself more comfortable in it. An example of verbal pacing:

"Do you realize we just met 10 minutes ago and already we're telling each other all this stuff? It's amazing how two people can just connect like this."

"Wow, we've been sitting here over coffee for 5 minutes and already we're talking about all these deep things. It's great."

"Hey, we just met here on the street and we're having so much fun already!"

7. Demonstrating "Cool Vulnerability"

Demonstrating cool vulnerability means showing a woman the lighter side of yourself. When talking to a woman a lot of guys try to come off like they're totally cool and never screw up, do anything weird, etc. Although it may SEEM to them that they're demonstrating value to her by doing this, most of the time they'd show even MORE value by revealing their human side. Now, you do NOT want to be revealing negative or aberrant aspects about you, like your tendency to wet your bed or your bad habit of punching through glass windows when you get angry. Instead, show some quirky aspect of your personality that is endearing, but not degrading. Lock the skeletons in your closet!

When I want to demonstrate "cool vulnerability" to a woman, I tell her about how I just CAN'T leave my car until a song I like has finished playing on the radio. I tell her how sometimes I'll be late getting somewhere, but I STILL just sit in the parking lot for 2 or 3 more minutes until the song is over. If I don't, I feel CHEATED out of the rest of the song. YES, this is weird, and a little uncool, but it's a quirky element to my personality that's endearing and shows that I'ma normal person just like her. Doing this is more important when you've heavily attracted and qualified a woman, since she might be intimidated by you by the time you reach the Rapport phase. By revealing vulnerability in a cool way, you disarm some of that intimidation.

You can also use embarrassing stories to demonstrate cool vulnerability. Just make sure that the situations you're talking about could've happened to anyone, and you handled them in a cool manner. You don't want to tell an embarrassing story that makes you look like a total dumbass, like the time you drank your face off in a bar and then shit your pants in the taxi ride home. NOT cool!

8. Using Indirect compliments

An indirect compliment is a compliment not about something specific, but instead compliments generally. It's a compliment that says that you like (or at least approve of) the same things she does, which of course is a way to demonstrate a connection between the two of you. Some examples of indirect compliments:

"You have a great sense of style" "You like a lot of great rock bands"
"You liked movie X? You have great taste in movies"
"You like X food? You must have a good sense of culture"

"You like X beer? Wow, a woman who knows her drinks!"
"You like football?? Women who're into sports are so cool!"

Try to be as general as possible. Saying "You have great taste in shoes" compliments her shoes. But saying "You have a great sense of style" compliments her ENTIRE style and holds more meaning for her.

9. Dealing with Awkward Silences

It's very important to deal properly with awkward silences. An awkward pause in the conversation means a break in rapport, and that your ability to connect on the topic is temporarily exhausted. You have to deal directly with the silence and attempt to reconnect on the topic later (or find something else to connect on by asking some more open-ended questions). Here are some ways to deal with it directly:

Full Guide to Being Cocky and Funny

1) Defuse the situation with humor: "Oh no, an uncomfortable silence! Don't panic, it'll pass". Then as she laughs, think quickly of a way to get back on the connection topic, or of an open-ended question to ask her.

2) Look the girl in the eye and ask, "I was wondering...From your point of view...What was it that made you say yes when I asked you out?" (or "What made you stop and talk to me when I approached you?" for a street or bar approach). She'll then go into how attractive you are, how sexy, how intelligent, successful, well dressed, impressive, etc. She is answering all of her "why not" questions before she even gets to the point of asking herself, "Why not this guy?" On a subconscious level she will feel more connected to you and feel like she really made the right decision by going out with you instead of some other guy. Be sure to use
the pauses in this statement, and ask the question slowly. This gives some context to the pause you two just hit (i.e. you were just getting ready to ask this question... right?). Also, it'll make the pause less evident if you start speaking slowly and thoughtfully after it.

3) One great tactic for when you hit a silent point is to move to a different location. If you can't take her to a new location, go someplace (bathroom, get a drink, etc) and come back again. Going to a different location works at several levels psychologically (i.e. helps create a history and time distortion). It also helps you to find new things to talk about because you can comment on the new area, plus it buys time (as does going and coming back again).

Whichever method you use, maintaining eye contact throughout the silences is very powerful. Don't ever look down or laugh nervously when you hit a pause. Look her in the eyes, smile confidently, and use one of the above tactics.

10. Using Cold reading techniques

Cold reading involves telling a woman general statements about herself that she personalizes and accepts as valid and accurate descriptions of her. It's the technique that psychics and newspaper horoscopes use.

Let's look at the typical horoscope in the newspaper: "Today you'll be contacted by an old friend. At work you'll find yourself faced with a situation you've mastered before and you'll breeze right through it. Finances will play a part in your day."

Full Guide to Being Cocky and Funny

Let's be realistic; unless you live under a rock, the odds are that someone you've known for a while will give you a call or e-mail you (old friend). You'll pay a bill, receive a paycheck, or be thinking about your money situation at some point (finances). You'll also be faced with a challenge at work and you'll survive—since work is challenging to some extent (if a job were easy they wouldn't pay you to do it).

The reason people believe this stuff is valid is because the statements are so general that anyone can find a life experience to fit the statement. Everything gets filtered and interpreted through a person's worldview, and fit to their experiences. Using cold reading takes advantage of this and makes it look like you have deep insights into people's character. People tend to think of themselves as unique (even though they have many characteristics in common with other human beings), and therefore they won't see the generality in a cold read.

Cold reading is a POWERFUL rapport-building technique. When you "correctly" tell a woman something deep about herself when you first meet her, she'll find it profound and wonder how you can understand her so well.

Remember though what I said at the beginning of the section about being SINCERE in your rapport building. What you say has to be at least PARTLY true to be accepted, and for you to come across congruently. If she's a raging party maniac who talks like she's on speed (she very well could be), you wouldn't say to her "You strike me as the type of person who's really calm on the inside". It would be more appropriate to use a read like "You seem to be someone who loves life and gets an adrenaline rush from being in the middle of the action."

In any case, cold reading is NOT lying, it's simply a general GUESS based on some observation of her character or behavior. You can make a cold read out of almost any observation. Just use the right setup for it:

"You seem to..."
"I get the feeling that..." "Something tells me that..." "I just noticed that..."

You can talk about how there's a side of the woman that's one way, but there's another side of them that is its opposite: "You have such a little girl's smile; it's so innocent. But I can tell from your eyes that you have a sinister side to you".

Full Guide to Being Cocky and Funny

Talk about how at times she can be one way, but at other times she can be another way.

Talk about how on the outside she's one way, while on the inside she's another way.

Talk about how she appears one way, but in fact she's really the opposite way:
"I bet a lot of people think you're really mature, but I know better. I can tell from your eyes that you're really just a little girl at heart."

Here are some full examples:

"You know, listening to the way you say things, I can tell you're someone who sees the world through her emotions". She'll find this profound and wonder how you can understand her so well, even though this statement covers 99% of women.

"You seem to be the kind of person who when you really like someone, you want to spend all your time with them... (self-point). But when somebody really annoys you (point away from yourself), you want nothing to do with them." Applies to pretty much anyone, doesn't it?

To a girl with a life with very little accomplishment: "You have a lot of undeveloped potential" Anyone with a shitty life holds out hope that they're capable of much more.

To a girl who's free-spirited: "You often feel hemmed in by restrictions and limitations, and you like to break the rules"

"You never accept anyone's opinion, unless you think about it, and make it your own". Good one for stubborn, argumentative women.

"Your relationships with the opposite sex in the past have given you some trouble" Best used when the woman accused you early on of player behavior, or displayed man-hating behavior, etc.

"You're the sort of person who needs admiration and respect from people." Translation: You're an attention-whore. Suitable for a woman trying hard to impress with clothes or whatever (seeking validation).

Full Guide to Being Cocky and Funny

"You have a strong sense of justice. Law enforcement would be a good job for you."

"You're a physical type, I can tell… So in what other ways are you physical?" For physical, "tough" chicks

For shy women: " I don't know if anyone has ever told you this before, but I noticed something really interesting about you." SHUT UP AND WAIT for her response. "You're an observer." (What do you mean, I'm an observer?) "Well, you like to observe people…you're a people watcher, an eavesdropper." (answer) "The thing is this: there are two types of people: people who are observers, like yourself, and people who live in the moment…And I bet when you are truly having fun, you can stop observing and be in the moment completely."

"I'm about to tell you something about you that no one has ever told you…"

To a hot woman who's acting arrogant: "You don't have me fooled for a minute, dear." (What are you talking about?) "Well, I know that most men fall for this 'I'm beautiful and aloof and I get my way' part of your personality… but I know something that none of them know… that there's really another side of you. A side that none of THEM get to see. I'll bet you a dollar right now that I know something about you that no one who's only known you for 5 minutes has EVER known… <pause pause pause>… You may act tough, but you're actually EXTREMELY sensitive on the inside. If someone makes a negative comment to you, you might act like it doesn't bother you…but you'll think about it all the way home… I know that secretly you're as sensitive as a little girl… it's just that most people never get to meet that part of you…"

For club girl: "I know you go out on weekends with the mindset of "I'm never going to meet Mr. Right at a club, but it boosts my ego to have men paying attention to me by the dozens, and I like to have free drinks… and I love to dance with my girlfriends and be a tease… and I love the power of shooting men down while pretending to be annoyed by it… etc." Shows her you're onto her game!

Many women harbor contempt for their beauty. At a certain level, they're kept from living a real life and being closer to the real world simply because fewer and fewer people can relate to them in proportion to how 'beautiful' they are and make themselves. Addressing this topic when speaking to women is VERY powerful. "Beauty is a curse."

Full Guide to Being Cocky and Funny

If she's being cold or acting tough: "Some women may act tough, but it's an ACT...you see it on their faces when they sleep, that vulnerability and desire to be protected that comes naturally from being a woman...The innocent desire to find love one day, and live out the fantasies she had while growing up...That's what I love about women...underneath it all there's that endearing vulnerability... You don't have me fooled for a minute, dear."

The key to cold reading is to really start OBSERVING people. You can use canned cold reads all you want, but being able to point out something you observed personally on the girl is much more powerful.

11. Matching and Mirroring

Verbal communications are only one way to develop rapport. The above verbal techniques are very effective at building rapport, but BY FAR the most effective tools for developing deep report is MATCHING and MIRRORING. These techniques use non-verbal cues to forge a bond.

Matching is the art of adopting the girl's same tone of voice and her tempo/rate of speech, as well as body language. If SHE speaks slowly, you speak slowly. If SHE has a dry tone, you adopt a dry tone. By slowing or speeding up your voice to match hers, and adopting the same tone of voice as her, she thinks "This person's just like me". It also subconsciously puts her more at ease because her communication isn't in conflict with YOUR tone and/or tempo.

Mirroring is the art of imitating someone's body language. It involves adopting her posture, her gestures, seating position, stance while standing, and eye contact (including duration of eye contact). If she holds her glass up high, you hold your glass up high. If she leans forward, you lean forward. If she cocks her head to the side, you cock your head to the side. If she's expressive with her hands, you become expressive with your hands. Mirroring communicates to her on a subconscious level that the person she's talking to understands her. It's important not to follow her body language immediately, since she may pick up on it and think that you're mimicking her and mocking her. Instead, leave a 3- second lag between her body language changes and yours. For example, she takes a sip of her water, you wait 3 seconds and then take a sip of YOUR water.

Once you've developed deep enough rapport using these techniques, you'll actually be able to LEAD. The woman will begin to unconsciously mirror YOU. You'll take a sip of your drink, and you'll see her reaching to sip her drink a few seconds later, following you unconsciously.

12. Potential Problems in Rapport-Building

The Free Therapy Trap

If a woman is attracted to you, she won't tell you her problems because she'd be afraid of scaring you away. If you find she starts talking about her depressive disorder or her fights with her mother, still having feelings for her ex-boyfriend, etc. it means either:

1) The girl establishes rapport with people VERY easily and likes to spill her guts (this is quite rare in pickup situations)

2) You've gone way overboard into rapport-building territory, and you've likely wiped out any attraction you managed to build earlier on in the interaction.

Either way, at this point she's starting to see you as more of a "nice guy" or friend, and she's opening the floodgates for her emotional problems to spill out. If you find yourself at this point, you need to act fast to get off this expressway to LJBF-land. You don't want to end up as an emotional tampon for a woman, soaking up all her pain like a girlfriend with a penis.

The quick solution is to move on to the AMPLIFY phase as soon as possible, with an emphasis on Breaking Rapport. You can directly do this by saying (NICELY):

"You know what? I really don't want to talk about this topic. Let's talk about something else." This will break rapport immediately and might even get her to shit-test you, which opens the door up for more attraction techniques.

Or you can say it jokingly:

Full Guide to Being Cocky and Funny

"If we keep talking about this I'm going to charge you 200$ an hour for therapy. Do you have your credit card with you?"

"Don't you have any girlfriends to tell this kind of stuff to? Are you trying to turn me into one of your girlfriends??"

One potential downside of the joking approach is that she may actually THINK you're joking, and that you're not serious about not wanting to hear about her messed-up life. Some people are just too thick and/or self-centered to get the message. If this is the case, you can then go to using the direct approach.

Over and Under-Doing it

A skill you need to develop in rapport building is CALIBRATION. You need to "fine-tune" the amount of rapport you use to match the needs of the particular woman you're interacting with. With deep, librarian-type women you can leave out a lot of the attraction and break rapport infrequently. With superficial party-girl types you can almost leave it out entirely and break rapport frequently, as long as the rest of your game is good. Most women will be somewhere in between, so start with the middle-of-the-road approach and then adjust it from there depending on the reactions you're getting.

Calibration is a skill that comes mainly from experience talking to women. You have to be able to read their reactions and see if you're having the desired effect. If you break rapport and the woman starts giving you more indicators of interest, you're on the right track. If the woman starts to show indicators of non-interest, you're doing something wrong.

Closed Body Language

If a woman is showing closed body language, don't mirror her as it'll only make her believe that you two definitely won't get along. Instead, comment on it in a neutral way that makes her feel self-conscious about it:

If her arms are crossed, ask "Are you cold?" She'll become self-conscious about her body language and open her arms. If she's very stiff and tense, say "Relax, loosen up a bit. You look nervous."

13. Phase-Shifting to Amplify

The amount of rapport you need to build depends on the outcome you're going for, and the needs of the woman you're dealing with. For quick street or club pickups where you just want to get a girl's number, you'll only need a little bit of rapport—sometimes just an indirect compliment or a quick cold-read will be enough. For a kiss close, more rapport will be needed. Sex closes will generally require the most prior rapport. Bear in mind though that there are no hard and fast rules here. If the girl is sexually liberal she may have sex with you with very little rapport. Or you might find a girl kissing you within minutes of meeting you. This is because rapport is just one piece of the entire puzzle, and you might get away with a successful close without it. But why risk it? If you see her going for rapport, then take advantage of that and build that connection. Even if you don't, pitch in a cold-reading or indirect compliment and see what results you get.

Chapter 6

AMPLIFY

1. Breaking rapport
2. Increasing rapport
3. Initiating Playful Kino
4. Looping Back to Earlier Successful Themes and Techniques
5. Using NLP Patterns to Amplify Emotions
6. Phase-Shifting to Close

This phase involves taking the good feelings you've instilled in her during the Attract, Qualify, and Rapport phases and AMPLIFYING them to higher levels. It's crucial to have her good feelings at a peak before moving into the tricky Close phase.

There are several strategies to amplify, and it depends on the situation and on how you've calibrated the woman's current state.

1. Breaking and Re-Establishing Rapport

After establishing rapport, and building it a bit, BREAK rapport by using an attraction-building technique (C&F, push/pull, takeaways, an open loop, etc). Then re-establish it by using a rapport-building technique. This is a great formula for attraction because it's like an emotional roller coaster for the girl. Think of a roller coaster: It starts off with a thrilling loop (C&F), then a straightaway (rapport conversation), then another thrilling sharp turn a bit later, etc. If it was all loops or turns you'd get annoyed (not to mention sick), and if it was all straight track you'd get bored. In the case of a male-female interaction, breaking and re-establishing rapport builds tension.

Full Guide to Being Cocky and Funny

A personal example to illustrate: After some attracting and qualifying I asked a woman what she did for a living (rapport-seeking), and she told me she was in marketing for a pharmaceutical company. I acted freaked out and joked, C&F "You're a DRUG DEALER??" She went red and said "Noooo! I market cardiac drugs!", and I came back with "You sell drugs to heart patients?? That's even worse!!" (extending the C&F theme) I then went serious and said "No really, that's interesting. What's involved in that?"—a sincere question to build rapport again. This is an example of a break/re-establish rapport cycle. Stacking several of these cycles together can be very effective.

Another way to break rapport is to sarcastically "force" rapport. "What's your favorite color?" She says Red. "Red? I like BLUE!!! Oh my God, we both have a favorite color!!"

One more way to break rapport is to tease her about things she mentioned to you during rapport building—like an evil form of "captioning". If she revealed to you she works in a day care facility and told you how much she hates changing diapers there, you can start teasing her by calling her "Miss Poopy Pants". Later, you can re-establish rapport with an empathy statement, saying how the one time you changed a baby's diaper it was a traumatic experience, and you can understand how awful changing them several times a day would be.

2. Increasing Rapport

Breaking rapport may not always be the wisest choice. For women who really crave rapport, your best bet may be to amplify that. There are several ways to do this.

1) One is to pull out every rapport building technique in your arsenal. Lay it on heavy with the empathy, cold reads, and matching & mirroring.

2) Another way to amplify rapport is with rapport building GAMES. The Cube is one of them. It's rather technical to learn, so read through the whole

description in the book "Secrets of The Cube" by Annie Gottlieb.

I'm not a big fan of The Cube myself. To me it's like a personality test, so in my eyes running The Cube on a woman is like pulling out a personality test from Cosmo and doing it with her. It's fun, it gets her talking about herself, but it's not YOU. If you were to use cold reading instead, she'll see YOU as a deeply insightful person. Feel free to use The Cube, however I prefer the other techniques for building rapport.

Another game useful for amplifying rapport and even kiss-closing is Soul Gazing. Ask: "Have you ever heard of soul gazing?" (yes or no) "Really? It's something they teach in Tantra. It's where two lovers stare deeply into each others eyes to really become in touch with each other. Wanna try it?" Follow with eye contact with bedroom eyes for as long as possible, if she starts to giggle then move in and kiss her. Soul-gazing works best when you've developed a lot of rapport already, and on girls who are more into woo-woo New Age stuff.
3) NLP patterns are another way to amplify rapport. NLP patterns are described later in this section.

3. Initiating Playful Kino

"Kino" is short for Kinesthetics, i.e. physical touching and body sensations. Playful kino involves tickling her, slapping her hand for being "naughty", flicking her ear or her hair, picking her up, throwing her over your shoulder, whatever. It's being physical in a playful, non-sexual way. Of course it could always get sexual later (in the Close phase), but for now you want her to associate good feelings with physical contact with you.

"Cavemanning" is another word for playful kino. Read more about Cavemanning in the Attract phase.

You can also bring up touch sensitivity to initiate playful kino: (she blushes at something) "You're a blusher?? Do you find your skin very sensitive to touch?

 # Full Guide to Being Cocky and Funny

Like if I ran my nails down your back slowly and gently, would it send electricity throughout your body?" If she says yes, run your nails down her back and smile. If she says no, say "We'll see" and do it anyway.

If she seems free-spirited, DO PHYSICAL STUFF THAT'S FUN: Make her spin around and ask her if she knows how to DANCE (this on the street). Make her TEACH YOU HER DANCE MOVES right there on the street. Grab her and start Salsa dancing on the sidewalk to her while making your own music. String some unrelated Spanish words together and make a song out of them as you dance with her.

Once you've had a good round of playful kino with her, use this: "I need to tell you something. This is serious. I'm pregnant. Our reckless (hand-holding/dancing/wrestling/whatever) has had consequences. I hope that you'll want to be a part of our new child's life, but either way I'm keeping it and there's nothing you can do about it. I'll be waiting for the monthly support check. You can start now by getting me something to drink. Oh my God, I just felt it kick! Hurry on that drink. Our baby needs it."

4. Looping Back to Earlier Successful Themes and Techniques

If something worked to attract her earlier, it's going to work to attract her now. If open loops were what really drove her crazy during the attract phase, then start several during this phase. Whatever it was, push/pull, C&F, role-playing, sexual themes, bring it back and really pour it on to get her heated up. After the calm period of rapport, bringing this behavior back will show a marked contrast, and it'll have an even greater effect than it did before.

5. Using NLP Patterns to Amplify Emotions

The idea of using neuro-linguistic programming (NLP) patterns for seduction comes from a method known as Speed Seduction. SS was pioneered by Ross Jeffries, and is probably the most well-known method in the seduction community. Using vivid, descriptive language, voice tonality, and subtle movements to capture and lead a woman's imagination is what it's all about. It's essentially low-level hypnosis, with suggestive "imbedded commands" scattered throughout the patterns.

The effectiveness of SS is hotly debated in the seduction community today, and even Ross Jeffries is gradually moving away from patterning to a more holistic approach to seduction, focusing on mastering control of your own state. Nevertheless, NLP patterns have been effective for many people over the years, so I've included a few here.

NLP patterns really heavily on tonality and languaging, so in most cases they're a poor choice of tool to use in bars, clubs, and other crowded and loud venues. However, over a cup of coffee, or in any quiet environment really, they can be pretty useful. Pick 2 patterns that you like best from each category below, memorize them, and practice them in the shower and while shaving over the next couple weeks. Then field-test them, and if you find they work for you, learn some more.

Pattern Guidelines:

* Speak slowly and clearly
* Lower your voice tonality (speak from your chest)
* Look her in the eyes while saying them (SOFT stare)
* Give a SLIGHT emphasis to the words in capitals. These are the "imbedded commands"
* Don't become attached to the pattern. Be prepared to drop it if the conversation shifts. Stick to short patterns when possible (especially with younger women from the MTV generation).
* Save patterns for isolation, when the woman is alone with you. On a busy street or with her friends is not a good idea since there are too many distractions.
* Work the pattern into the conversational framework so it has some relevance to what you're talking about. Don't just start reciting it out of the blue. Learn to steer conversations towards patterning.
* SP is an abbreviation for Self-Point. A self-point is a visual anchor made by

making a subtle gesture towards yourself, so slight that only the woman's subconscious will pick up on it. Practice self-pointing in conversation so that it truly becomes natural and subtle.

A couple of the patterns below were authored by me. However, most of them I've adapted from the original SS materials, and shortened considerably. If you'd like to learn the original patterns, or learn how to make your own, consult the various Speed Seduction materials available on the market.

Patterns for amplifying rapport

INCREDIBLE CONNECTIONS pattern, short version: "You know how you can just talk to someone [self-point] and no matter how long it's been you JUST FEEL THIS great connection with them..." (That's cool, I have a friend like that) "Someone you can really trust, who always makes you feel good to talk to? [self-point]" (Yeah, I've known her forever blah blah)

INCREDIBLE CONNECTIONS pattern: "You know what I find is so interesting, is how with some people you just don't connect at all [point away from yourself], and with other people you just FEEL AN INCREDIBLE CONNECTION [self-point]. Like when you start to LISTEN CAREFULLY and REALLY LOOK AND HANG ON EVERY WORD, it's like the rest of the things around you just start to disappear, and the entire world becomes THIS FACE YOU'RE LOOKING AT [point at your face!], THIS VOICE YOU'RE HEARING...that's when YOU START TO FEEL THIS INTENSE CONNECTION."

PEAK EXPERIENCES pattern: "Do you remember the last time you had a peak experience? Like climbing a mountain, skydiving, FALLING IN LOVE? WITH ME, [self-point] I find that they make life worthwhile. It's those times where something gives you that RUSH [self-point], and your heart beats faster, and you FEEL AMAZING."

Patterns for establishing a love connection to you (extreme rapport)

WAIT FOR DATE PATTERN: "Have you ever been waiting for someone [self-point] to pick you up for an evening, and all of a sudden you hear that knock on the door, and your heart leaps...You FEEL the adrenaline rushing through your body, and the closer you get to that door, the more you feel the butterflies...and then when you open the door it's like WHAT YOU WANT THE MOST IS RIGHT HERE [self-point], RIGHT NOW, RIGHT IN FRONT OF YOU."

FASCINATION PATTERN: "I haven't had that Butterflies feeling in a while. I mean the feeling where I get out of bed and the first thing I want to do is call her...I don't mean sexually, I just walk into a club and I'm thinking "Ok, her, her, her [point at her], her, and her"...I get butterflies in my LOINS a lot, but not in my stomach in that puppy love way...When was the last time you were just, FASCINATED with a guy? (sp) I mean just totally taken? When he was stuck in YOU'RE MINE, and the more you try not to think about this guy the more you actually DO think of him? (sp)

LOVE AT FIRST SIGHT PATTERN: "You ever wonder why you just FALL IN LOVE AT FIRST SIGHT? What's it like when you JUST DO THAT? NOW, WITH ME [self-point], I think what happens is that a lot of things go on deep inside you and you're not even aware that YOU CAN'T HELP YOURSELF. NOW, it's kind of like a switch [make clicking noise and flick her ear up] goes on in your head and IT JUST HAPPENS...WITH ME [self-point], I think that's just how IT HAPPENS. Kind of like a light turns on in your body and just glows, you know?" Best used when she complains about how she can't find a good man. Tell her "You'll find one, he may show up any minute now!", then talk about love at first sight and segue into this pattern.

FALLING IN LOVE pattern. "Do you remember the last time you fell madly in love? I bet I can tell you how that happened!" (her: blah blah) "You spent time with that person [self-point] and then you went home, and you PICTURE THAT PERSON'S FACE IN YOUR MINE! [as you do this, draw a frame around your own face] Right?" (her: blah blah) "And then, maybe you IMAGINE YOURSELF in all sorts of situations with this person [self-point again] having lots of fun?" (her: blah blah) "And then maybe you start to list all the qualities about him you really like: He's so smart, he's so funny, he's so fun to be with?" [self-point] (her: blah blah) "And then, here's the worst part...You start saying his

Full Guide to Being Cocky and Funny

name out loud, you start bringing it up in conversation with your friends, and maybe you even dance around the house, singing it like a goof? That's when you know YOU'RE ABSOLUTELY HOOKED on someone [point to her solar plexus]. You know what I mean?"

ROMANCE NOVEL PATTERN: "My friend was saying that for her, it's almost like she has these categories of men...and it's kinda funny how in some ways, it's almost like different types of BOOKS. Some men are like encyclopedias. They are always there...always where you can see them or know where they are... They are the standard way of looking up information. You know they will never probably be off the shelf for long. No one really ever borrows them, they are just there, and you'll BE SECURE in the fact that it's up there for you when you need it [motion away from you while explaining this category]. Then OTHER men are like magazines. Fun, fluff, they're like buddies. No real content. They're always around, show up regularly, you check them out when you want a distraction from the everyday world. [motion away from you while describing this category]. And then, there are other men...and THIS type of man [self-point] is more like a Romance Novel. You know, those books where on some level, you enjoy this, you really like to allow yourself to enter this fantasy...to have this experience [self-point]. And the thing with a romance novel is, it's an ESCAPE. It's something where you know that this will only be around for a while, and that's ok [self-point]. You know that there will be a time for you to really get into this...and really let this get into you...and then you'll let it go...and enjoy this even more [self-point]...I think the complete woman is one that embraces all of these "books". And knows what to expect from each." Long, but if you can get through this one and paint yourself as "the romance novel", it could be useful.

Patterns for amplifying sexual feelings and attraction

CELEBRITY REDIRECT PATTERN: "What singer or actor do you find really sexy, WHO REALLY ATTRACTS YOU?" [self-point] (Her answer) "(repeat name)? And what is it about THIS GUY [self-point] that really turns you on?" [self-point again] (Her answer) "What would you do if he were here, right where I am right now?" [self-point] "Would you JUMP HIM?" Get her all hot and bothered, and with the subtle self-points you direct those feelings towards YOU.

THE LARONDE PATTERN: "I was watching the Learning Channel last week. They were talking to people who design rides and attractions for amusement parks like LaRonde. Wouldn't that be a cool job to have?" (yeah) "Well, they were talking about the things that make up the ideal attraction [self-point]. First, when you EXPERIENCE the ideal attraction, you FEEL A STATE OF HIGH AROUSAL. The ideal attraction makes your heart beat faster, and your breathing gets faster and you just FEEL THAT AMAZING RUSH ALL OVER. And then they said that another part to an ideal attraction is it's fascinating. You just FEEL SO EXHILARATED that you want to TAKE THIS RIDE [self-point] multiple times. As soon as you GET OFF you want to GET BACK ON AGAIN." (continue point) "And the most important thing they said was a sense of overall safety. That even though the attraction might look a little dangerous, YOU'RE CERTAIN YOU'RE SAFE...YOU FEEL SAFE because you realize nothing bad can really happen, so that lets YOU FEEL TOTALLY FREE TO LET GO AND ENJOY IT again and again. Anyway, it was a good show." Best used if she hates her job or is complaining about it. Talk about cool jobs, etc. then mention the people that design amusement park rides.

SURRENDER PATTERN: "Have you ever just sat back and ALLOWED yourself to be seduced? I mean without games, without the chase...Just sitting back with a guy [self-point] and letting go, and giving total control to THIS GUY [self-point]? It's been said that women are the gatekeepers of sex, they decide who goes in and out, literally...but that can be a heavy responsibility...if you were to JUST LET IT GO and SURRENDER that power, to me [self-point]...in my view...that would be very liberating. Best used when having a conversation about her playing "hard-to-get", or liking to play games, or playing guys in clubs, etc.

REMEMBER SEX PATTERN: "At least you can always relive your past sexual experiences in your head! What's it like for you when you REMEMBER INCREDIBLE SEX? Do you FIND YOURSELF GETTING HORNY as soon as you FLASH BACK TO IT? Or do you find you need to REPLAY IT IN YOU'RE MINE...and SEE THE SIGHTS...and HEAR THE SOUNDS...as if YOU'RE THERE...WITH ME I find I have to do the replay to really GET DEEP INTO IT. What about you?" Best used when you've already talked about sex a bit, and you're now talking about her lack of it!

SATISFACTION PATTERN: "Women are sexual creatures. They have 3 basic needs: They need to be SEDUCED, they need to be EXCITED, and they need to be SATISFIED. I think SATISFACTION is the most important. A woman will still be happy with a guy who's lousy at the first two, but knows how to satisfy her. It all comes down to satisfaction. What satisfies you, (her name)? A quick lick across the back of your knee, or a long, sensuous lick from your achilles tendon to the back of your neck? Or maybe something a little more animalistic have more of an appeal?" Used to get her hot and bothered if you've got the signal that she's interested.

6. Phase-Shifting to Close

When should you phase-shift into closing the woman? When you can tell that you have her "amped up" to the point where you have a good chance of success. It's as simple as that.

Chapter 7…last chapter guys

CLOSE PHASE

1. Taking the Lead

2. Contact Closing

3. Kiss Closing

4. Meet Closing

5. Sex Closing

6. Ejecting

The term "closing" comes from sales, where it's used to describe making the final sale of the good or service to the client. In pick-up and seduction it describes getting what you want from the woman, be it a number, a kiss, a meeting, or sex.

When attempting a close of any kind, the most important thing to do is RELAX! When you realize that you don't have to close all the time, then it takes the pressure off and you become much more relaxed. Paradoxically, this almost always leads to your closing far more often than you ever imagined possible!

The key is to KEEP GOING AND CONTINUE TO THE NEXT STEP ALWAYS. If your conversation is going well, do a contact close. If you're out for a walk and the conversation seems to be going well, do a kiss close. If you're at your house watching a movie and you start kissing, take her hand and lead her to your bedroom for a sex close. Keep advancing! Women like this and expect it. If they're not comfortable, they'll tell you about it. But don't worry. Just keep going, and advance again at next opportunity.

There's one thing about closing that you MUST keep in mind. If someone won't give you what you want, no amount of begging, pleading, arguing, guilt-tripping, or logical arguing is going to make them give it to you. You need to focus on changing her MOOD rather than her MIND. If she's reluctant to give you her number, get her laughing, develop some rapport with her, then attempt another contact close. If she's not ready to have sex with you, then rev her up with teasing and anticipation and try again later.

1. Taking the Lead

Sometimes you may have a woman all wound up to the point where she actually volunteers her number to you. Sometimes she'll invite you out somewhere, and occasionally she'll kiss you without any prompting on your part. RARELY she'll be the one to initiate sex with you. But the reality is that most women are PASSIVE and YOU, as the man, have to take the lead. YOU have to be the one to approach, to get the number, to arrange the meeting, and to make the move to kiss her or bed her. That's just the way it is. It's in most women's natures to be submissive, and they want a dominant male to LEAD them through all these steps.

If you find yourself complaining that women should be the ones to approach you, to ask for your number, to jump on you and kiss you, or to start grabbing your crotch to get sex, GET OVER IT. This is the way it is in our society, and in fact in most of the animal kingdom. You're going to HAVE to stick your neck out and risk being rejected, and you'll just have to deal with that reality. Just like you won't meet many women unless you go out and TRY to meet them, you won't get a kiss or a sexual encounter with a woman unless you make an attempt to get it.

The good news is that once you've passed any of these steps with women, they tend to open up and initiate it a lot more themselves. They'll come up and kiss YOU, or drop to their knees while you're watching TV and do wicked things to you. They just want YOU to be the one to initiate these things the first time.

One important corollary of the man being forced to take the lead is to EXPECT RESISTANCE. At every step, even if a woman really likes you, she'll put up resistance. No girl likes to feel like she's "easy", and no matter how much she wants to give you her number, kiss you, or have sex with you she'll throw up some barrier or objection to convince herself that she at least TRIED to resist you. This resistance is known as the ASD, or anti-slut defenses.

2. Contact Closing

Contact close involves getting a woman's contact information from her. This means either her e-mail address, her home phone number, her work phone number, her wireless phone number, or any combination thereof. Whichever of these is best is open to debate, and depends really on your preferences and on the woman.

If she's always at work then the work number would be a surer way to reach her, but she may be too busy to talk. This can work in your favor actually, because you can talk to her just long enough to schedule a meet and then get off the phone. But if you have good phone gaming skills and want to keep her on the phone for a while, this is bad.

If she's a heavy social type and always out of the house the wireless phone would be the best bet to reach her. The downside to this is that the sound on them is usually horrible, she'll be either out with friends or driving when she answers, and probably very distracted. Again, bad for phone game.

E-mail is generally safe in that it's less intrusive and a woman will give it up more easily. With a phone she doesn't have much choice; it rings, she answers, and she's put on the spot talking to you right then and there. But if you send her an e-mail, she can answer it at her leisure, or block you from contacting her if she decides she doesn't really like you.

Closing Fluff

You can set up a contact close by using fluff talk which leads to it. Here are two examples:

(She's telling you something) "I have to go now, but tell me all about it some other time! While I'm massaging your shoulders for example!" (rub one shoulder and give her a preview) Give me your number so we can continue this later."

(Look down at your watch) "Okay, I talked to you for two minutes, AND I let you shake my hand...That'll be twenty dollars, tip not included". (response) I really have to get going, I'll collect my money the next time we see each other." (start to walk away) "HEY! Do you have email?" (segue into contact close)

Getting her contact info

Full Guide to Being Cocky and Funny

Remember the rule, "Never ASK a woman for anything". Don't say "Can I have your number?" Instead say "What's your number?" or use soft commands like "Give me your number." Don't be worried about looking pushy or forward, since if a woman wants to give you her number, she'll give it to you either way. It just sets the whole dynamic up better if you don't "ask" for it.

Below is a pretty easy and proven way to get contact info:

"Well, it was nice meeting you. I'm going to get back to my friends/whatever." Then, just as you're turning to walk away, and you kind of disconnect, turn back and say "HEY! Do you have email?" If she says "yes," take out a pen and paper and say "Great, write it down for me" and have her write it down. Then AS SHE'S IN THE MIDDLE OF WRITING, say "Put your number down here too." (this works more than just going for her number outright, as she's already in "yes" mode while giving you the e-mail). As she's writing down her phone number say "Is this a number that you actually answer?" If she looks at you and hesitates, or says that it's her "voicemail or pager number," then say "Look, write your REAL number down. It's going to be OK, I'll only call you nine times a day." If the answer to the email question is "No, I don't have email" then bust on her and say "Well, do you have ELECTRICITY?" Then say "Well, OK then...I like email better, but just give me your number. It's so damn hard to reach people on the phone these days."

Here are some C&F ways to contact close:

"Let's do xxx together. I'll call you" (But you don't have my number) "Oh that's right!" (pull out a pen)

"You know what? I think I'll make you my new girlfriend." (Uh... what?) "Yeah, I just decided that you'd make a nice girlfriend for me." (blah blah) "Ok, tell you what... I will make you my FAVORITE girlfriend. Give me your number." (if she won't give it) "How can you be my favorite girlfriend if I don't even have your number?"

(If she accused you of trying to pick her up earlier) "Ok, now I'm OFFICIALLY picking you up. What's your number?"

"Well... now that we've set up a meeting, there's a question you need to ask me." (What?) "Oh come on!" (What's your number?) "See I knew you'd catch on! Let's exchange numbers."

"You can't leave...You haven't given me your phone number yet!"

Full Guide to Being Cocky and Funny

(If things have gone really well) "So are you gonna give me your phone number, or do I have to stalk you?"

Pull out your cellular phone, and start looking it over curiously. "I wonder how this strange device can help us continue our conversation later. SURELY there must be a way…If only we could unlock its mysteries…"

Group number-close: The ultimate way to number close two or three or more women that are all beautiful and interesting is to say "You know, you guys are EQUALLY DORKY, so instead of just rejecting all of you, I'll let you all give me your numbers, and maybe we can hang out sometime…And I can teach you how to be cool like me"

Post-Contact Close Concerns

If you suspect that she might have given you a fake number, when she gives it to you fluff-talk for about a minute or so. Then say "Okay I gotta go" and look at the number. Then say "Tell me your number again? Just to see if I'm reading it right" If what she gives you doesn't match, it was bullshit! Call her on it, or even better, crumple it up and flick it at her, saying "Never mind, I don't want it." Which is true, since you're dealing with a flake anyway.

If she treats it like giving you her number was a big deal, you can say C&F "Wow, I'm HONOURED to have been given your sacred trust…Your phone number is a sacred thing. I feel like someone has just given me their virginity."

Lastly, when you do the contact close, don't just trade numbers. Accompany it with a humorous "But when I call you, I don't want you to answer "Huh? Who? Ah… its you… uh… so… howzit going…" I want you to act really enthusiastic and happy, like "Oh, you called! God I'm so glad!!", ok? Is that a deal?" Additionally you can end the phone call in the same manner: "So when we meet, I want you to smile, give me a big warm friendly hug and take my hand. Deal?"

Contact Close Resistance

If she's reluctant, or outright refuses to give you her number, you NEED to use C&F. You want to change her mood so that she relents. Here are some comebacks:

"Don't worry! I'm only going to call you nine times a day. I'm not one of those CLINGY guys."

"What? You give your number to the pizza guy when you order a pizza, right?" (Of course) "Great. Give me your phone number and we'll order pizza ogether."

"Oh, C'mon! Lower you're standards a little. I did..." (Not the best line to use because it conveys lower social value, but a good last ditch effort)

Often a woman will ask for YOUR number instead. This is a brush-off because remember, women are PASSIVE and won't call unless she's really impressed by you (in which case she'd give you her number anyway, right?). Here are some rebuttals to "Why don't you give me YOUR number?":

Direct: "Don't give me that crap, give me your number."

"Look, I'm not that easy. Let's EXCHANGE numbers."

(Give me YOUR number) "I know how you women are! You collect phone numbers and brag to your girlfriends about them and have little competitions and throw them away once you've had your ego boost." (No, not me, protest) "Okay, then prove me wrong and write down your number".

If she REALLY refuses to give out her number, proceed with one of the following:

"I'd still like to get to know you and I think you should get to know me before you pass judgment."

"Well now that I've gone to this much trouble the least you could do is talk with me on the phone."

Of course those two statements really set up a poor frame (that SHE'S the one giving YOU a chance), but they beat walking away with nothing. If this works to get her number, be sure to turn the frame around as soon as you can after you have the number.

If things have REALLY gone poorly and none of the above troubleshooters have worked, try this as a last-ditch effort:

"Just so it's not a total loss, do you have any cute and single friends who are available?"

For all you know, she may have an entire army of hot friends she could introduce you to. You could turn this "loss" into a huge potential gain!

3. Kiss Closing

If you can read body language fairly well, you'll know when the girl is receptive or ready or even waiting for a kiss close. She'll let you touch her without resistance, touches you in return, wets her lips slightly and/or looks at your lips, especially when you are about to leave each other. But there are a number of situations, where

Full Guide to Being Cocky and Funny

The Bet Kiss Close

Tell the girl that you'll bet her a dollar (or a drink) that you can kiss her without using your lips or your tongue. Girls usually think/know that you're up to something, so sometimes it takes a little convincing to get them to take the bet. They'll take it about 1/3 of the time. If the girl is a good friend and she doesn't take the bet, say "Ok. Fine...Just check out this trick I learned...you can use it to make money off people," then play it off like your doing her a favor by showing her this. Then if she accepts the bet or you offer to show her "the trick" do this: Say: "Ready...Watch this!" Then move in like you are going to kiss her on the lips. Ok this is important. When you reach the point of no return you absolutely MUST lay the smoothest and I mean the smoothest kiss on her she has ever experienced. Then say "Damn you're a good kisser! I guess I owe you a buck!" If your kiss is smooth enough this will most definitely lead to more kissing and maybe even a child! (If you need a good C&F line here say "I don't think that kiss was worth more than 50 cents, you owe me another")

The 10-Scale Challenge Kiss Close

"On a scale of 1-10 how good of a kisser are you?" They'll usually say a ten (hot chicks want to sustain their value as a hot chick). Then kiss her. Why does this work? This works because you're challenging how good of a kisser she is. After it's done, say C&F "That was terrible! Let's do it again to see what you've REALLY got!"

The Hug Kiss Close

Best used at the end of a meeting/date, if you haven't kissed yet. "Well, gimme a hug, because it's way too soon for a first kiss." Hug her, then say "Well now that we've successfully passed the hugging stage, we can kiss."(kiss her!)

The Playful Kino Kiss Close

Playful slap kiss close: When you're teasing each other and she makes a bratty comment, slap her leg just a LITTLE too hard. When she complains, go to "kiss it better". Then look her in the eyes, smile and say "I hope I don't have to slap your lips to get a REAL kiss". Then kiss her.

The No Sex Kiss Close

If a woman hints at sex with you, or the topic of sex comes up: "I couldn't have sex with you just like that...I don't even know if you're a good kisser yet!" Then move in and kiss her.

The Eyes Closed Kiss Close

Full Guide to Being Cocky and Funny

Ask her to rate her kissing skills on a scale of 1 to 10. When she asks you how good of a kisser YOU are, say "I've kissed so many women I can do it with my eyes closed. Watch." Then move in to kiss her.

The Kiss Description Kiss Close

"You know what the perfect kiss is? It starts way before your lips meet--it's this little knot in the pit of your stomach. Then it flashes in your eyes, giving the signal for both of you to move in. And what's more intense sometimes than the kiss itself, is that moment right BEFORE the kiss...When your lips are almost touching and you can feel the electricity...as if we're kissing the air between us..."Move in very slowly as you're saying this, timing it so that when you say "kissing the air between us" your lips really ARE just separated by a tiny space. Kiss her as soon as you've finished saying it.

Kiss close Statements of Intent (SOIs)

"You have the lips of a woman who knows how to kiss a man."

"You realize, of course, that you and I are gonna be kissing later". Say this with a dead serious look on your face.

"I want to get a movie and go to your house so that we can pretend to watch the movie while sexual tension builds until we start making out like animals in heat."

"I'm trying so hard not to kiss you right now".

She asks "Do you want to kiss me?" "Not as much as you want to kiss me."

Dealing with Kiss Close Resistance

Most kiss close resistance will be caused by either:

1. YOU appearing unsure of yourself

2. The presence of friends (remember the ASD!)

3. Insufficient attraction and/or rapport built earlier in the encounter

4. She just flat-out finds you "unkissable" (not her type, your lips are all cracked, you're sick and she doesn't want to catch it, etc)

Obviously #4 you can't really do anything about, but for #1-3, the solution is to take a step back and do what you were doing before, FIX whichever of the three blocked you, then attempt to kiss close again.

Full Guide to Being Cocky and Funny

Don't show anger or hurt at having your kiss close rejected. Smile and joke about it C&F: "Geez, you sure know how to spoil the mood, don't you?". Or say in a sarcastic yet charming way, "Why did you tease me if you didn't want to kiss me? You're a very bad girl for trying to play games with me. I'll bet you tease all the men you meet." This way you can always try again later, whereas if you'd reacted to it badly you probably would've blown all your chances for a future kiss close.

Two-set kiss close

YES, you can kiss-close a two set, if the girls are adventurous and/or bisexual.

"Which one of you is a better kisser?" If one says "ME!" take her up on it and kiss-close her right there. Then say "Well, that was good, but let's see how she is". Then you go and kiss-close her friend. It's totally congruent with the conversation, so it's the natural thing to do. "Yeah, that was good too, but I'm having trouble deciding. Let me see." Then go back and kiss the original girl again, then the friend to compare. Point to the least hot one and say to the hottest one, "SHE's the best kisser." After this the hottest one will probably try to prove her value and pounce on you, kissing her very best. If things are going well, "She's pretty good, kiss her and see". If you're with the right kind of women, they'll kiss each other and you can say "See?" Bring up "Have you guys ever had a 3-way kiss?" then kiss one immediately after the other. At any point in this game if either of the girls acts weirded out or prudish, say you were just playing around and make fun of her for taking you seriously.

4. Meet Closing

Ok so you've done everything right and contact closed the woman (or even kissclosed her). Now you want to set up a meeting to see what she's about, and possibly take things further.

There's no rule that says you have to go home and call her to set up a meet close. You can do it immediately after you've met her, by saying C&F: "Do you think you could keep me interested enough for a cup of coffee?" and then taking her to the nearest coffee place.

Dating

Now most people would probably refer to this meeting as a DATE. Try as much as possible to avoid saying or using the word "date", and to stay out of the dating frame. This is because "dating" puts two people in a special context. The typical "dating" relationship has the guy taking the girl out, paying for everything, doing nice things to win her approval, etc. until the woman decides if he's worth sleeping with or not. You want to stay out of this frame and avoid it like the plague, because you set up that SHE is the prize and you're after her. You want to approach the situation with YOU as the prize, or at least on an equal level as her.

"Dating" can also be quite expensive. By the time you've bought flowers to bring, got your car washed and gassed up, paid for dinner and wine at a nice restaurant, and taken her out dancing at a club and paid her cover and drinks, you've EASILY spent over $100. Or let's say you want to take her on one of those "original" dates that dating experts recommend, like bungee jumping together or white water rafting excursions. These activities can cost upwards of 80$ per person (Canadian Dollars), which can get ridiculously expensive. Consider even a "simple" date like going to the movies. With movie ticket prices hovering around 10$, and the cost of goodies at the concession stand being so outrageous, you're spending a good 40-50$ for a night out.

Now, if you're out meeting several attractive women a week, and manage to set up a date with 2 or 3 of them, how long could you sustain this rate of spending? (As an aside, this is what men are complaining about when they say that having a girlfriend is expensive, or when asked why they don't date more say, "I don't have the money to do it"). And why would you want to spend all that money on people you don't even know yet?

On a first date, why does a man take a woman out to dinner? Is it to evaluate her table manners and watch her chew her food? No, it's to give her pleasurable feelings through good food and atmosphere, and have her link those feelings to HIM. Why does a man take a woman white water rafting? Is it to get her shirt wet so he can see her boobs? No, it's to get her to have fun and excitement and link those feelings to HIM. And why does a man take a woman to a horrible "romantic comedy" at the movies? Is it so he can watch Julia Roberts trip over something a dozen times, and play hard-to-get for the whole movie and predictably give in at the end? Of course not, it's to get the woman he's with all emotional and happy so she'll link those feelings to HIM.

Let's be honest here. Doing all of the above is MANIPULATION (though most women don't tend to think of it as such, because they're so used to it). And it's pointless! When you've left the fancy restaurant, when you're driving home from the rapids, or when you leave the movie house, it's just going to be YOU. So instead of using EXTERNAL elements to influence how a woman feels about you, how about just demonstrating what YOU are all about? If you're a fun and interesting person, then just sitting on a park bench and talking would be a lot of fun.

Full Guide to Being Cocky and Funny

I'm not saying that you can't take a woman to dinner or spend money on her. If you want to do that that's fine, but only AFTER you've come to know her and see that she's worth it. Remember, your frame is that YOU are the one evaluating her, to see if she's up to your standards. Whenever you make an effort to try and prove something to her (i.e. qualify yourself to her), you reverse that frame and she'll be the one in control. Women don't want to have all the control in courting—it's the man's job to lead with a strong frame!

Gold-Digger Shutdowns

Beware of a woman who EXPECTS or DEMANDS that you take her out on expensive dates. Nothing gives her away as a GOLD-DIGGER faster! If you find a woman saying something like "You're going to take me to (expensive restaurant) this Friday", say "You know what? I don't think this is gonna work out. I barely know you and you want me to spoil you, that doesn't make any sense." Really, even if you DO have a large amount of discretionary income, this is NOT the type of woman you want to get involved with.

If she talks about deserving it because she's beautiful: "You're in MY world now. Your looks don't get you a free anything".

If she talks about having expensive tastes: "If you have expensive tastes then you need a If she talks about being "high-maintenance", deal with it using one of the responses to the high-maintenance shit-test in the Attract section.

Whatever the case, know the signs and avoid these leeching types—nothing good can come of them (except maybe an affair with her while she dates or marries a boring rich guy to satisfy her lust for cash!)

First Meeting Options

Ok, so we've established that it's a bad idea to take women out on expensive sorties. So with that addressed, just what do you do on a first meeting? Here are some options:

1. Meeting for coffee or tea: This is probably the best option, because cafés are relatively quiet (no blaring music), private (there are corners, booths, etc), and in most places it's self-serve so you don't have a waiter interrupting you just when her buying temperature is getting "up there". Cost: Under 8$

2. Meeting for drinks: You could meet her in a bar or lounge for a drink or two and some conversation. The pros of this are that with some alcohol in her she may be more playful and of course, horny. The down side is that she may be drunk when you

arrive (she may have had several drinks bought for her by other guys before you got there). Also, the music is likely to be louder in these venues, and you'll have a tougher time gaming her. The biggest drawback is that there'll likely be AMOGs present, and you'll have to go through the hassle of deflating their advances on your girl, or plow through them to get to her if she arrived at the venue before you. Cost: Under 10$ if you don't stay long and each have one drink.

3. Meeting in the park: If it's a nice day, you can meet her on a bench in the park, or even have a picnic together if there are any tables set up.Show up with some sandwiches, wine glasses, and a bottle of Lemon Perrier (public consumption of wine might get you a ticket). Cost: Under 10$

4. Bring her shopping: By this I don't mean taking her out to buy her stuff. I mean saying "Hey, I'm going shopping for X tomorrow, you can come along and give me a female opinion". Cost: Nothing over what you would've paid to buy X in the first place.

These are just some basic ideas. If you want any more you can check out "300 Creative Date Ideas for Under $20" by Michael Webb, available for download online. In any case, more ideas may be redundant because you should know by the 2nd meet if she's worth pursuing further or not.

When to Call

Once you have an idea of what you want to do, you'll need to contact her to invite her to meet. How long should you wait after you've met her before calling? Opinions differ on the mandatory waiting period but most say 2 to 4 days. This is because most people approach the question with the mindset of "How desperate am I going to look if I call after X days?" This is the WRONG way to look at it. If you didn't come off as desperate or an ass-kisser when you met her, you won't look like one when you call her, at ANY time.

In reality it depends on how much rapport you two built during your initial encounter. If you feel you built heavy rapport it means you can take longer, and light rapport means you'd better not wait too long. If you met her in a club environment, the flakiest environment known to man, you should call her as soon as the clubs close. This may seem counterintuitive, but she may barely remember you 2 days from then (especially if she'd been drinking) so do it. Call her wireless at closing time and try and get her to meet you at the 24-hour café downtown, the all-night diner, the after-hours club, a sleazy motel, whatever. (Just kidding on that last one).

However long you take, if she seems annoyed at how long you took, or that you didn't call her when you said you would, say C&F: "(name), I'm a GUY. We NEVER call when we're supposed to!"

A note on calling: Nowadays, with voicemail boxes, answering machines, caller ID, *69, etc., trying to get in touch with a woman can be like a campaign of technological warfare. Here are some ground rules for dealing with the new technology:

* Always assume the girl has caller ID. If you don't have a private number, before calling use *67 to block your number from her. If you don't, and you try 5 times to reach her throughout the day, she may think you're a phone-stalking psycho.

* If you happen to get a machine when you call, hang up and call back immediately. The rationale behind this is that often the woman will be standing right next to the machine ready to screen the call, and by hanging up she gets frustrated because she wanted to know who it was. As she starts to walk away the phone rings again, and to ease the frustration she'll go to answer the phone this time.

* If the above strategy doesn't work, call back a little later and leave a message like this: "Hey X, this is Mike. I just had the most AMAZING idea... you have to hear this! Call me, 555-1234".

This should get her to call back. She will of course ask what the idea was. Say "I figured out how I could get you to call me back. It totally worked too... Hey, you won't believe what happened to me yesterday... [story]"

Setting up the Meet Close

The objective when first calling her is to get to know her a little better and set up a face-to-face meeting. Don't talk too long—10-20 minutes will do. Try to get her to see you as soon as possible—it cuts down on her flaking. You should always be "semi-ready" to go out when you first-call a woman; that way if she says she's not busy at the moment you're good to go.

The plan is to

1. Call her

2. Make her laugh or engage her interest within the first 5 seconds

3. Use the Attract-Qualify-Rapport-Amplify parts of the plan to raise her interest

level again (15 minutes MAXIMUM—do NOT linger on the phone for hours)

4. Meet close

5. Hang up

When calling, don't get into the dead end of trying to remind her who you are over and over until she gets it. Instead, state who you are and where you met and plow right into your phone game. "Hey, it's Mike from Club Exit. Check this out, the coolest thing happened to me after I left there..." That way, even if she doesn't remember she'll be so into you that she'll probably show up for the meet regardless. If you get stuck trying to remind her, she'll just keep saying "No, I don't remember" and hang up. If you barrel through it whether she remembers or not, then she'll get into you and you'll bypass that. Also, trying to remind her of who you are takes you out of the powerful frame that YOU are the prize. When you act in that frame you assume that there's no way she could possibly forget YOU and that she remembers you perfectly.

Run your game on her and run a meet close before ending the call.

Executing the Meet Close

Get her involved and invested in the outcome. Planning what you're going to do when you get together increases her involvement and increases the likelihood she won't flake. Here are some examples of how to bridge to the topic of a meeting:

"So when are you taking me out? No McDonalds either...I wanna be WINED and DINED! And no cheap night at the movies!" She'll laugh at this, then you turn around and say "Never mind, I wouldn't feel comfortable with you spending so much money on me. Instead we'll do   . Sound good?"

"We should get together this week. Come with me to   on Xday."

"Well I'm busy on Xday, Xday, and Xday afternoon, how about Xday in the early evening? Just say YES." (show you're busy and your time is valuable. If she already has plans that night) "You already have plans? CANCEL THEM! I'M more interesting!" She probably won't, but just suggesting that she cancel them for YOU sets you up as the prize.

"I'm busy tomorrow, but if you tempt me with a good enough offer, I might make time for you the next night".

The Tag-Along Meet Close:

The tag-along meet close is used when her buying temperature is low (for whatever reason, the phone can be tough) and you want to communicate that you're not needy: "I'm going to X with my friends tomorrow, and you're welcome to come along if you want."

Meet Close Potential Problems

If she rejects your offer, she may just be busy with plans she can't break that night. Offer a maximum of ONE more night that you have available. After that if she says she's busy, and doesn't suggest another night herself (a sign that yes, she actually does want to meet with you), say:

"It's ok, I hear ya. (PAUSE) What I DON'T hear is a counteroffer. Make me one! (Doesn't:) You know, it doesn't sound like you're serious. That's too bad, because you seemed cool...anyway I gotta go make plans, I'll talk to you later." Then hang up. Say it without sounding hurt or angry; just state it matter-of- factly.

It's important not to rule out women who turn down your meet requests. Never burn your bridges unless she's a total loser or bitch! Maybe she's just having a bad day or she's tired, maybe she's dating another guy, maybe she's on the rebound, etc. What you need to do is put the women who turned down your offer on a call-list. Every two weeks go down the call-list and call all the no-girls, repeating the process again and trying to meet-close. This is good for two reasons: First, it shows persistence, in a COOL way. You're not calling her everyday, hanging on and trying desperately to get her to see you. Second, it'll make her think that—imagine this—you actually LIKE her and you're not just out for a quick lay! A lot of girls are worried about this, and they may keep a guy at a distance until they're confident he's not just out to love 'em and leave 'em. You really have nothing to lose by trying her number again in a couple weeks. The worst she can do when you call her up is be unenthusiastic and tell you she's too busy to talk.

When you successfully do a meet close, you're not home free yet; you may be tested by the woman. Here are two examples you might see at meet close:

* "Where are you taking me?" She assumes you're "taking her" somewhere—she's trying to assert the dating frame. Your response, C&F: "I'm not "taking you" anywhere, we're meeting for coffee, remember?"

* "Call me on Xday to confirm" This is a woman's "escape hatch"— don't let her get away with it! Basically it means "Ok, I'll go out with you that night...UNLESS someone makes me a better offer". Your response, C&F: "Confirm? Confirmation is for CATHOLICS. Coffee at X on Xday it is!" From here move right into flake prevention strategy.

Full Guide to Being Cocky and Funny

FLAKE PREVENTION: "Now, let me ask you something: On a scale of 1 to 10, what are the chances that you're not going to show up on Xday?"

If she answers with anything more than "0", say:

"You know what, never mind. If there's even a CHANCE that you're not going to show up, I'm not even gonna go. One of my pet peeves is people who cancel at the last minute or stand me up. I don't do that to people

because it's a matter of keeping my word...because if there's one thing that could end our friendship before it starts, it's flakiness."

Let that sink in, then continue:

"I'll tell you what, the place is close to my house, so just meet me at my place, ring the bell, and I'll come out and we'll go. That way if you're late or stand me up at least I'll be at home instead of sitting in the place like a dork."

Another method of flake prevention:

When setting up the meet close, ALWAYS say something like "I'll call you if my plans change, but otherwise I'll see you at X." This takes the LEAD, letting her know that YOU will be the one to change the plans, NOT HER.

Ending the call

When everything's settled, say C&F: "Great! It'll be cool for us to hang out together. Being seen with me will be good for your reputation."

When getting ready to hang up, say "It's gonna be fun to get to know you better. You'd make a cool friend." (friendship frame surprises and disarms her and puts less pressure on you at the actual meeting). This doesn't mean she'll slot you in the "friends" category though, far from it. It makes you look non-needy.

5. Sex Closing

"Women want to get laid as much as men do. They just want it about 15 minutes later than we do. So hold out for 20 and she'll be chasing you for 5." –from the film, The Tao of Steve

It's important to qualify a woman's sexual interest and openness to sex as well as her conditions and time line for doing it. When you know where she stands you can act accordingly and not stab in the dark thinking she needs more touching, another meeting, or perhaps more sweet words whispered in her ear.

It's important to have a strong frame and lead her using it. Don't think too much about making a move, just do it. Let your instincts take over. Don't look for signs. If she's sticking around with you or kissing you, THAT is the sign. If she's in bed with you, THAT is the sign. Once you see the above signs, do whatever it takes to have consensual sex with her. If she is not going to have sex that night, she'll let you know firmly. Otherwise, seal the deal. But you'll never know unless you try.

Try to use ANTICIPATION to great effect. Get her hot and bothered, then pull back. Do something else to get her hot and bothered, then pull back. And just when you know that she's really enjoying what's going on (and it can be at any stage, kissing, etc.), just STOP. Then whisper in her ear "You want more, don't you?" (yes) "You're going to have to say PLEASE." Or if she says "Make love to me/fuck me", you respond "I'm not finished kissing you yet".

Resistance to sex

If you ever FORCE a woman into a sexual act against her will, you deserve to be thrown in jail and have the same thing done to you!!! When a woman gives you a firm NO, it means NO.

That being said, there's a difference between a firm NO and "no.....I can't......no...... Make love to me!!!" This sort of weak, token resistance to sex is very common. Before we can understand it (known from here on as Last-Minute Resistance/LMR), we have to understand where it comes from.

To begin with, what is a SLUT? To a Christian lady I know, Britney Spears is a slut because she shows her cleavage. To another guy I know, ALL women are sluts (except the one he's going to marry, of course). One woman I know (who's had over 40 sexual partners so far and commonly has sex on first dates) considers a woman who cheats during a committed relationship a slut. And another woman I know thinks it's "slutty" to have 3 or more sexual partners on rotation at one time (2 is okay though).

My point is that unless you adhere strictly to religious teachings, what constitutes deviant sexual behavior is a matter of opinion. The word "slut" is subjective to the point that it's meaningless. Yet every woman fears being seen

as a slut! With no defining point, it's impossible for a woman to set defining standards for her sexual behavior, and she's always in doubt about it. This end result impacts our ability to sex close a woman.

Not only does a woman not want to be seen as being a slut, she doesn't want to see HERSELF as a slut either. Even when she's alone with you, you're bound to come against some resistance (though in some cases, TOKEN resistance) to sex, no matter how horny you've made her or how badly she might want you. The way to overcome that resistance is to give her an EXCUSE to have sex with you, something she can blame it on to take some "blame" off of herself. This is why a woman will have 2 beers and have sex with a stranger, then blame the beers for clouding her judgment. Or why a woman will backwards-rationalize a one-night stand, saying "Oh it was my cousin's friend's best friend's bachelorette party so it was a special occasion". In other words, she finds something to excuse her behavior.

One VERY powerful technique to disarm resistance is to paint it as YOUR responsibility. Her anti-slut defenses could be disarmed by you claiming that it's YOUR fault, and that she's just helplessly giving in to the moment—and that it's totally normal. Her excuse is—YOU!

Another technique is to actually AGREE to the resistance, de-escalate, then re-escalate again later when she's more comfortable. For example, she moans "Noooo don't touch me there..." and you say "You're right, I shouldn't be touching you there" and you take your hand away. Then you do other things to get her even more hot and bothered, and then you go to touch her there again, finding no resistance this time.

Another way to get through the resistance is to illustrate that it's all in her head. Here's PlayboyLA's red light/green light routine for getting through resistance:

PB: You're a study of opposites

HB: What do you mean? I just don't know you well enough yet...

PB: Of course – but two people never really know each other – and besides, you and I both know that there's part of you that wants one thing, and another part which wants another.

HB: (Shrugs) Whatever PB, maybe so

PB: There's this, which clearly wants one thing (taking her hand – which had been jerking me off), there is this which wants the same thing (pointing to her tummy – meaning her emotions), and of course this, which clearly wants the same thing (touching her pussy, which was warm and wet)...but, then there's the almighty THIS (pointing to her head)...which wants the opposite. (She giggles here)

(So, I'm pacing her reality and showing a real understanding of her inner world).

HB: (giggling) Yes, you're right...

Full Guide to Being Cocky and Funny

PB: You're like a little car in stop and go traffic – so frustrating for the better drivers out there. It's "Red light" (point to head) "green light" (point to hand) – "red light" (point to head) "green light" (point to tummy) – "red light" (point last time at head) "green light" (point to crotch, stay there...)

This had her giggling, really at herself, so I re-escalate this time and each time she stops me I say "red light" and flick her head (slightly painful) while smiling, and each time she allows me to proceed I say "aaah, thank you for the green light"...this pacing and leading routine accompanied with reward/punish has worked a number of times for me. One resistance tactic a woman is likely to use on you is the Time Concept: "I've only known you 2 days/1 month/whatever". For this you can run Style's "No Expectations" routine:

"I don't go into an interaction with expectations in mind... I dated a girl and we took 3 months to have sex. Another girl it was the first night, because it was immediately passionate. I liked both girls equally, because both just felt natural and didn't try to veer things in one way or another."

If resistance is persistent and seemingly unbreakable, the important thing is to show real indifference to having sex with her. Women tend to validate their appeal through their sexual desirability, and when a woman knows a man wants to do her she's fulfilled that need and knows she "has him". But when you at least act indifferent to actually sleeping with her, the only way she can validate her desirability is to sleep with you.

"Fine, you and I aren't having sex. We're going to be friends". MEAN IT. Don't kiss her, cuddle with her. Just be cool like you would be with a guy friend. In this case if she has a strong need for validation she may backtrack and start pursuing YOU. Especially when you had this fun, flirty dynamic before her refusal—she'll want the good times back.

"I'm not 16 anymore, and I don't like girls who are flaky and who don't have the guts to go after what they want.".

"You know, you can't always get what you want. You should be familiar with the territory"

"Sex is both parties abandoning themselves to the moment. You can't abandon yourself in the moment if you still feel you need to protect yourself. That's why TRUST is important. Do you trust me?"

"It's good not to expect something to happen, and just let everything go the way it goes." Steal this frame before she does, if you need to.

At first these might look like mind games, and they are! But they're not malicious. What you're trying to do is NOT "trick" her into having sex with you; at that point she already WANTS to! What you're trying to do is break down a couple decades' worth of social programming that's preventing her from seeking her own pleasure (and you'll just happen to get some out of the deal too).

One thing: It's important that once she's comfortable, try not to change the location if at all possible. If she's now comfortable in your car, your room, etc., try to seal the deal there. A change in location could make her lose the state she was in, the ASD could kick right back in, and you could lose control.

Other ways to get her comfortable

I hate to state the obvious, but unless you plan on fucking her in front of others, isolation is key. Get her somewhere secluded so that she doesn't have to worry about people finding out.

After you've brought her to your place, go to the washroom. It gives her a chance to look at her surroundings, hear the music, look at the décor, etc. She'll become more relaxed and comfortable in your environment.

Humourous/Suggestive Sex Closes ("Is he joking or serious?")

"My expert opinion is that you have the perfect body for a night of wild love making."

"I have two bottles of champagne at home. One to drink and one to pour all over your body..."

You're at her place, and she apologizes for her place being so messy "Hey, I'm a GUY. I'm not looking at the stuff on the floor, I just want to add the stuff you're wearing to the mess..."

"I'd love to take you home and do things that the Lord forbids."

"Why don't you surprise your roommate and not come home tonight?"

"Do you like having your neck bit? (Why) Because right now all I want to do is bite your neck."

"Personally I think between YOUR dirty mind and MY dirty mind, we'd make a WICKED team..."

Full Guide to Being Cocky and Funny

"I really love smart women...I think they're more fun, they're sexier, they're better in bed... A smart woman would never turn her back on a good thing... Unless it's for a MASSAGE!"

"What are we gonna do? Well we can play the ALPHABET game! You don't know what that is? Keep it that way, it'll corrupt you." (Get her to beg before you explain) "Ok, the alphabet game is a game you play with a naked woman. You lay her on her back, spread her legs, and then draw the entire alphabet on her sex with your tongue."

"Do you know the difference between a hamburger and a blow job? You don't? Well in that case, do you wanna have lunch together?"

Asks question: "I'll tell you later in bed."

"I think I could fall madly in bed with you."

"It would be dangerous for us to get involved anyway. What if we really HIT IT OFF and get married and have kids? Then in a few years we could get divorced, and the kids would be caught in the middle! So I think it's in the best interests of the children that we keep any relationship between us purely SEXUAL. THINK OF THE KIDS, (her name)! THINK OF THE KIDS!"

"I think it's important for a girl like you to have someone keeping her "happy". It's tough, you know...CELIBACY IS A HANDS-ON JOB! I know it's not easy!"

"I'm MAD at you. Let's get into a HUGE argument." (Why??) "So we can have INCREDIBLE make-up sex after." (heehee) "Actually, we don't have to have an argument for that."

OVERT Sex Closes

On a date, look right at her, and say, "You know at this point in the evening, I know there's some guys who would lean forward, look right at you and say, "I'd like to take you home right now, and fuck you like you've never ever had it before!" Now, IF she lights up, her pupils dilate, and she maybe even says, "YEAH!", then you know what to do! If she looks put off or upset you say, "But I know YOU require a much more sensitive, and subtle approach from me."

"I want to lay you down and kiss you from head to toe and back up again".

"I want to explore every inch of your body with my hands and lips. I'm intoxicated with just the thought of being with you, emotionally and physically. If I was alone with you right now, I'd just want to melt right into you..."

"I have some questions for you". (Go ahead) "How long has it been since you had an incredible massage? Since a man licked your neck and your whole body trembled? Since you felt a man's saliva on your clitoris?" (answer) "Come with me and we'll shorten that time considerably".

Other Guy objections ("But I'm already seeing someone")

In cases where she's already "seeing" (fucking) someone else, you can use standard boyfriend destroyers from the Find/Open section, or one of the following.

"Oh that's too bad, I feel bad for you..." (Why?) "Cause while that guy's reading the sports page, I'm reading a book on how to give a woman a a better orgasm...or Sex Games. But that's okay, stay with what you've got..."

"Does he satisfy your needs all the time, or only when he senses YOU'RE BORED WITH HIM?"

After-Sex statements

"Thank you for sharing your body with me." (for emotional women, don't use this with a party girl or fuck friend)

"That was so good I think my neighbors need a cigarette".

"You made a good impression on me...Your claw-marks on my back!"

6. Ejecting

Ejecting comes from fighter pilot lingo, and means to escape from a crash and burn. Another term for ejecting is "Null Closing", closing your interaction with the woman or set without achieving any real objective.

Don't linger! End the interaction on a high note and eject if a sex close isn't likely. This leaves a possibility for future interaction, whereas if you wear out your welcome the bored woman will eject you herself (not good). You also demonstrate that you're not desperate and have other things to do with your life. Besides, you may have better luck with the next one! Here's an example ejection phrase suggested by Mystery for use in a club/bar situation: "The night is young... pleasure meeting you". If you strike out, say "It's been a real pleasure meeting you". Say it like you really mean it - in a friendly, respectful, yet empathic manner. This way you'll set yourself apart from all the losers who leave mumbling "bitches, they're all the same..." You'll remain cool, confident, a gentleman in good humor. And she'll feel crappy after realizing SHE just lost YOU! Or if she has simply ignored you, add "...didn't realize you were deaf"

14279991R00110

Printed in Poland
by Amazon Fulfillment
Poland Sp. z o.o., Wrocław